PAPER
CRAFT

NORTH
LIGHT
BOOKS

ACKNOWLEDGEMENTS

PHOTOGRAPHS:

Ariadne Holland 61, 63, 64; Bridgeman Art
Library/Victoria and Albert Museum 84; Jon Bouchier
25; Sarah Colegate 97; Country Times and Landscape
1,77; Cy de Cosse inc 49(br); Dorling Kindersley/Steven
Hayward (from *Malcolm Hillier's Flowers*) 33;
Eaglemoss (Tif Hunter) 95, (Martin Norris) 10, 12, 50,
57-60, 78(b), 103-106, 121, 122, 124, (Zed Nelson) 98,
(Simon Page-Ritchie) 34, 131-132, (John Suett) front
cover (background), 8, 19, 27, 32, 52, 65-68, 73, 74, 87,
88(t), 93, 102, 107, 125, 127, 128, 129, (Steve Tanner)
front cover (inset tr,b) 2-3, 13, 16, 20, 21-23, 41, 43, 53,
56, 89, 90, 104, 109-110, 111, 117, 120, 135, 141-142,
(Shona Wood) 39-40; Robert Harding Picture Library 6;
Hobby Origami/Falken Verlag 139; Modes et Travaux
front cover (inset tl), 35-37, 51, 69, 72, 76, 92;
Schmoller Collection 81; Tony Stone Worldwide 46(tl);
ZEFA 46(tr,bl,br); 100 Ideas 7, 9, 17-18, 26, 29, 31, 47-
49, 78(t), 85, 86, 88(b), 113, 115, 116, 134.

ILLUSTRATIONS:

Louise Bruce 36-38, 122-124; Teri Gower/The Gallery
28, 70-72; Kevin Hart 14-15, 18, 20, 22-24, 34, 40-42,
54-55, 59-60, 66-68, 82-83, 86-88, 90-91, 98-100, 110,
112, 126-128, 130, 132-134; Sally Holmes 48; John
Hutchinson 62-64, 74-76, 140-142; Bill le Fever 44-46,
94-96, 136-138; Stan North 10-12, 30, 104-106, 114-116,
118-119; Tig Sutton 79-80.

First published in the USA in 1993
by North Light Books,
an imprint of F&W Publications Inc.,
1507 Dana Avenue,
Cincinnati, Ohio 45207.

1-800-289-0963   88610

Manufactured in Hong Kong

CONTENTS

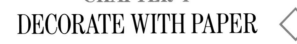

CHAPTER I
DECORATE WITH PAPER

CHAPTER II
PERSONALIZE WITH PAPER

CHAPTER III

 # CELEBRATE WITH PAPER

CHAPTER I

DECORATING WITH PAPER

◇

Mounting pictures

*Picture mounts are the 'in between' areas
between the frame, or the edge of the glass, and the picture.
They can have elegant, bevelled edges,
mitred corners with border trims or use any number of
imaginative ideas as decoration.*

A typical picture mount is made from card and cut out as a 'window frame' to surround the image, to help display it, and to set it back slightly from the glass.

To work well, a mount should help the eye concentrate on the main subject, the picture, without distracting attention from, or overpowering it. That is not to say that all mounts need to be plain neutrals, or nondescript. Mounts can be anything but boring; besides making a picture look more interesting, as shown with the ideas for treatments of cheap prints on the

△ *Subtle colours and textures are a clever way to enhance black and white photographic prints.*

following pages, they can be interesting in their own right and still enhance, rather than compete with the picture.

Choosing the proportions

If a picture is mounted centrally, it often appears out of balance. This is an optical illusion and to compensate for this, mounts are cut with a slightly deeper border at the base. Usually an extra ½in (1.2cm) added here is sufficient to balance the picture.

It is useful, before cutting a mount, to lay the picture flat and to place a larger piece of paper, with a window cut out to the same size of the picture over this. Move the glass (or frame if there is one), over the paper to find the position that best suits the colour and size of the image. Pencil round the glass, or inside the frame, to mark the proportions for reference. Transfer the marks to the mount so you can cut it accurately.

Different colour mounts

Colour can affect proportions and the way we see them, so it is important to choose (or decorate) a mount in a shade that keeps a good balance with the picture.

The most successful picture mounts are those in colours that link in some way with the artwork. For instance, if the colouring is mainly warm, then a mount will look best in a toning, warm shade. Likewise, cool colours would look best against a cool-coloured mount.

Dramatic colour contrasts can also work with great success. The picture would have to be quite bold for this to work well: a striking black and white print can look marvellous set against a mount in a bright primary colour like red or blue. Likewise, colour opposites like blue and yellow, or red with green, used together as picture and mount offer another bold option.

Do not be afraid to experiment with colour, but consider the setting in which the picture will hang, and choose colours that are pleasing to the eye.

Materials and equipment

Mounting board (mat board), or card, can be bought at most art shops or graphic suppliers. Take the picture with you if possible when choosing a mount, so that you can select the best shade for your picture. Mounts can be made from one sheet of card, or from two sheets, used as a double mount, or from a combination of card and layers of paper. You will also need a piece of card as a backing for the picture.

Mounting board is available in various textures and thicknesses but ¹⁄₁₆in (1.5mm) is usually suitable for most needs. If you intend mounting an unusual piece of work, something bulky or valuable, it is wise to ask advice about suitable materials beforehand.

A heavy duty craft knife is needed to cut the card, and to cut the bevelled 45° angled edge which gives a professional finish to the window cut in the mount.

A bevelled edge cutter is designed to cut at a set angle.

A straight metal edge, such as a long ruler, is used to cut against, and when drawing lines. A large set square is used for drawing accurate corners.

You will also need fine glasspaper (a type of sandpaper) for smoothing down the surface on the cut edge of the card; a piece of mounting board and a piece of wood to use as cutting surfaces (these should be longer and wider than the size of the finished mount); a sharp pencil, two small screws – for steadying the work on the surface – and a screwdriver. Low tack aerosol adhesive, masking tape and stick adhesive are useful for holding pictures and mounts in place.

▽ *Assemble the materials before you start: pictures, mounts and frames, together with adhesive and cutting tools. The yellow, bevelled edge cutter is only worth buying if you have a lot of work to do.*

Cutting a mount

1 Start by measuring the outside size of the mount. This will be the same size as the glass if you are using a clip frame. Draw these measurements lightly on the right side of the mounting card, using a ruler and set square.

If the picture is to be framed, rather than held behind glass with clips, measure the depth behind the inside edge of the frame, down to the rebate level. This measurement is incorporated in the mount size.

2 Cut the outside edge of the mount. Place the mount under the straight edge, and resting firmly against this, cut the mount along the drawn lines as described.

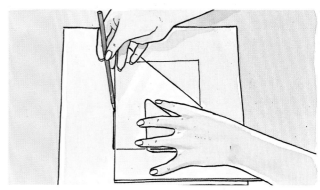

3 Using a set square and ruler, mark in the window position, allowing a wider border at the lower edge. Allow for a margin of at least ¼in (6mm) to overlap the artwork. Check that all corners are right angles and lines are parallel.

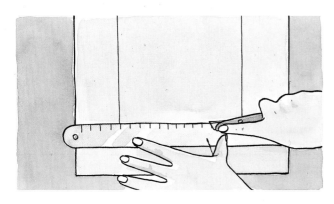

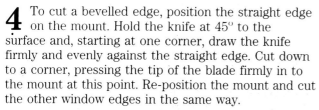

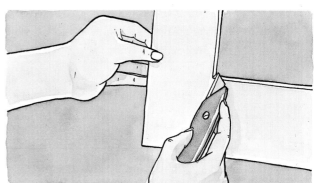

4 To cut a bevelled edge, position the straight edge on the mount. Hold the knife at 45° to the surface and, starting at one corner, draw the knife firmly and evenly against the straight edge. Cut down to a corner, pressing the tip of the blade firmly in to the mount at this point. Re-position the mount and cut the other window edges in the same way.

5 Carefully remove the centre of the card and check the corners. Use the tip of the knife to clear away any card debris which might have been left in the corners of the mitres. Use glasspaper to smooth the edges and corners of the mitre cuts.

TIP STEADY SURFACE

To prepare a cutting surface, partly work two screws into a piece of wood, and rest the ruler against these. Use a piece of mounting board, as a mat to cut on, under the straight edge. Slide the card mount in position, under the straight edge, and cut, holding the knife firmly and pressing against the straight edge. Make each cut over a different piece of board so the surface is always smooth.

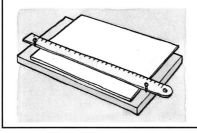

Mounting a picture

1 Place the picture on a surface, so the lower edge of the picture overhangs slightly. Position the mount over the picture. Hold the mount and picture steady with one hand, or weight with a suitable object. Reaching under the edges of the picture and mount, attach one or two pieces of masking tape to hold the two together.

2 Turn the mount over, and secure the top edge with masking tape. Carefully remove the pieces of tape from the other end. The mount is now ready to be framed.

Adding borders

Ready-bought wallpaper borders are useful decorative additions to plain mounts. They can be used with bevelled edge card mounts, or to dress up a simple mount cut from paper. Mitre-cut corners give a professional look and are easy to make. Few designs will meet exactly at the corners, but the general impression will be acceptable.

To mitre a border

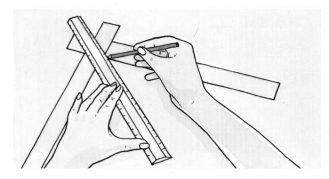

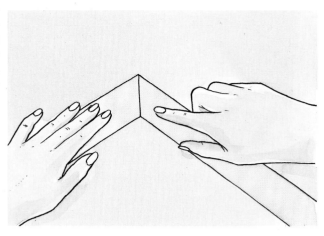

1 Cut two lengths of border, longer than your needs. Place them across each other at right angles. Check the angle with a set square and check that the pattern matches effectively. Place a ruler diagonally across the borders and draw a light pencil line.

2 Cut across the overlapping border and re-align it to the other piece. If the paper is very fine, the underlap can be left in place, otherwise, the corners are butt joined. Mark the underlapping border level with the overlapping edge and cut out.

3 All the corners are cut in the same way. Work the top two angles first, then measure the required size and cut the lower corners. Glue the borders in place on the mounting board. A stick adhesive is useful for this.

Following a theme

Mounts can be effective when they follow a theme set by the picture. For instance, the nostalgic holiday poster postcard used below has a mount decorated with old railway tickets, which makes it an amusing picture, as well as a clever way of displaying a collection of souvenirs.

The wallpaper border (left), used as a mitred edging, blends beautifully with the picture, as the subjects are both flowers.

The oriental prints (below left) have been mounted on hand-made paper. The effect is reminiscent of a Japanese screen.

Pleated paper blinds

*Paper blinds can be as versatile
as the more familiar fabric variety and are surprisingly
durable. Even fine handmade papers can
be used; mounted over thicker sheets they still manage to retain
their delicate translucent qualities.*

Pleated paper blinds are ideal for small windows, although larger blinds can be made just as well — they simply require more sheets of paper. The blinds are made by folding paper concertina-fashion to the required width and depth of the window. The folds can be set close together as narrow pleats, or widely spaced as deep folds. They are held in place with a fabric 'touch and close' Velcro fastening strip attached to the window frame. To pull the blinds up and down a cord is threaded through pierced holes on each side of the blind, and through eyelet screws attached to a wooden strip on the frame.

Different effects

The simple operating system allows for plenty of scope with design variations. Paper can be cut, torn, perforated or applied as a controlled pattern, or a free collage to a supporting backing paper, to give the effect you want. The cords can be varied too.

Choosing papers

Oriental papers are an inspiration as their subtle colours and textures, enhanced when set against bright light, make them a natural choice when designing paper blinds. Japanese and other unusual handmade papers are available from specialist suppliers and art shops, and many are strong enough to use on their own. Other papers, like the beautiful but fragile cobweb paper (more usually chosen to wrap chocolates) used to make the blind pictured on the previous page, can be a practical choice if mounted over a darker, thicker paper which adds support, and displays the design to the best advantage.

Choose papers that crease well without cracking, so avoid surface coated poster papers and some foils. Experiment by pleating a selection of papers.

Materials and equipment

Papers Select enough sheets to cover the window area. Cover paper, similar in weight to cartridge paper (drawing paper), is ideal, and is suitable for backing fine or handmade papers.

Adhesives Use PVA adhesive (white glue) for joining sheets of paper together, and a spray adhesive, sold for mounting photographs, for bonding top papers to backing papers.

Artists' mounting card or similar weight card is used to strengthen the top and base.

Cord or **ribbon** is required to operate the blind.

Hole reinforcement rings are used to strengthen the holes.

Other materials needed are: a strip of wood as wide as the blind, ¾in (2cm wide); 'touch and close' Velcro fastening as wide as window; screw-in eyelets; a cleat hook; acorn light pull attachment; metal knitting needle and ruler, and a hole punch.

Measuring for the blind

To estimate for materials needed, measure the outside edges of the window. The width of paper should match the window width. Depending on the size of blind and the type of paper used, you may need to join several sheets of paper together to achieve the correct size. To calculate the depth of paper needed, add an extra one third to the window depth measurement, and adjust to the nearest figure which is divisible by 2¼in (6cm); this allows for pleats 1¼in (3cm) wide. Add 7¾in (20cm) for top and bottom edgings.

To estimate the amount of cord or ribbon needed, allow twice the length of the unpleated blind, plus twice the width, and enough extra to reach half way down the blind.

Joining sheets of paper

Joins between sheets of paper should be as unobtrusive as possible. They can be butt-joined on top of a backing paper; this is advisable when working with translucent papers, where an overlapping join would show. Alternatively, for heavier papers,

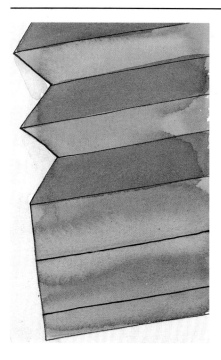

4 Starting at the top end, make concertina pleats along the score lines as shown, leaving the last two lines unfolded.

5 Cut a 1in (2.5cm) wide strip of mounting card to fit across base of the blind. Stick in place with PVA adhesive, enclosing card with the last two folds of paper.

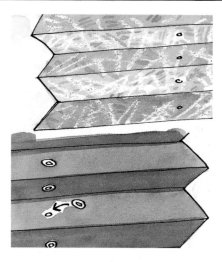

6 With right side of blind facing, punch a ¼in (6mm) hole through each fold, positioning the holes about one sixth of the blind width in from each side. Put a reinforcement ring on each hole.

7 With back of blind facing, score one line ¾in (2cm) down from the top edge and another line 2¾in (7cm) from the top.

8 Cut a 1¾in (4.5cm) wide strip of mounting card to fit across top of blind and glue in place as for base piece.

Paper blind

The instructions here are for a blind like the one shown on page 13.

You will need

◇ Daler cover paper in deep shade
◇ Translucent figured paper
◇ Mounting card (mat board or card stock)
◇ PVA (white glue) and spray adhesive
◇ Cord or ribbon
◇ Wooden strip ¾in (2cm) by 1¾in (4.5cm) by window width
◇ Two screw-in eyelets
◇ ¾in (2cm) wide Velcro
◇ Cleat hook
◇ Light pull acorn
◇ Hole punch
◇ PVC hole reinforcement rings
◇ Metal knitting needle, scissors and ruler

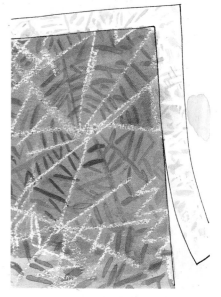

the join can be overlapped by the depth of a full pleat, or half a pleat. Arrange the joins so they occur on a pleat at the back of the blind; joins placed here will be less noticeable than along the front edge.

Use PVA adhesive to secure the joins, and leave the papers to dry thoroughly under a heavy weight.

1 Cut cover paper to size, making joins as necessary. Spray evenly with adhesive. Leave until tacky. Lay translucent paper on top, overlapping edges of cover paper. Butt join papers if required. Smooth papers in place.

2 Trim away the translucent paper, cutting it level with the edges of the cover paper.

3 Working from back of blind, and starting 4¾in (12cm) down from top edge, use a ruler and knitting needle to measure and score horizontal lines 1¼in (3cm) apart. The last line will be ¾in (2cm) up from base edge

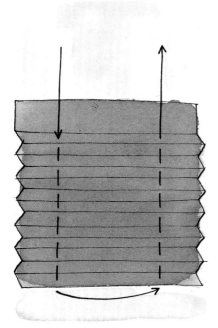

9 Thread cord down through holes on one side of the blind, across and up through holes on other side. Leave cord ends loose.

10 Cut wooden strip to blind width, and screw the eyelets in, ¾in (1.5cm) in from long edge. Position carefully to match up with the holes in the blind.

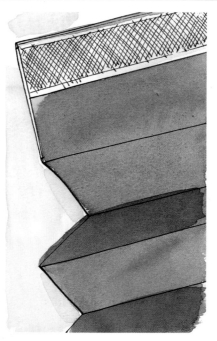

11 Glue hook side of Velcro strip to top of blind, and glue remaining part to wooden strip.

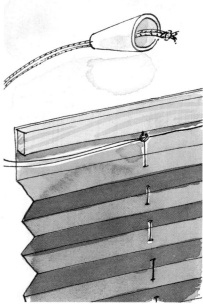

12 Screw wooden strip to window frame. To fix blind in place, thread cord through eyelets, then through acorn and knot securely.

13 Screw cleat hook to side of window frame and wind cord round to secure blind in position.

PATTERN LIBRARY

△ *Coloured parchment is mounted on cartridge paper then run over with a tracing wheel to produce a linear design of hundreds of tiny holes. Spotted ribbon makes perfect pulls.*

△ *Three shades of torn tissue paper are mounted in a random diagonal design on to a cartridge paper backing. The blind is strung with toning Russia braid.*

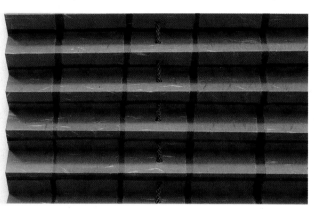

△ *This design is made by tearing squares of terra cotta paper against a ruler. The dark backing and matching cord give the design a simple sophistication.*

△ *Coarse string is a humorous accompaniment for a blind made from heavily textured handmade paper which is strengthened with a backing of cartridge paper.*

▽ *Brilliant gold cord pulls give the finishing touch to this blind made from white handmade paper mounted over cover paper, and decorated with torn strips of gold gift wrap.*

Novelty napkin rings

*Farmyard animals are an amusing theme for
papier mâché napkin rings. Each member of the family can
choose their own favourite animal and avoid
mix-ups with the table linen. The designs are modelled using
the simple paper strip and glue method.*

Mid-weight cardboard tubes cut into rings make the bases for the napkin rings, while the little papier mâché animals are shaped over moulds made from modelling plastic. Once the papier mâché has dried, paint the napkin rings in bright colours and cheerful patterns to capture the lively mood of a farmyard scene. The set includes a cow, a sheep, a rooster and a rabbit.

For more information on working this type of papier mâché and using modelling plastic, see pages 39-42, 43-46 and 61-64.

You will need
To make any design:
◇ Cardboard tube with a diameter of 2¹/₂in (6.5cm)
◇ Newspaper cut or torn into ³/₄ x ¹/₄in (2cm x 6mm) strips
◇ Wallpaper paste (without fungicide) mixed full strength
◇ Tracing paper
◇ Modelling plastic (modelling compound)
◇ Modelling tools
◇ Scraps of felt and ribbon
◇ Clear quick drying adhesive
◇ Fabric adhesive
◇ Poster paints or other water-based paint
◇ Water colour brushes
◇ Clear household varnish — gloss. satin or matt finish

Modelling the animals

The animals are shaped in modelling plastic and this is used as a mould for the papier mâché. Refer to photograph and diagrams when modelling the animals. Use the outline diagram as a guide for the shape and size of the animal. The areas marked with a dotted line are built up on each side of the main shape. Glue on the felt ears of the cow and sheep.

1 So that the base of the animal will be curved to fit the napkin ring, shape the plastic clay mould over a spare piece of cardboard tube, anchored to a piece of wood with a tack. Shape animals following diagram.

2 Grease the animal mould and cover it with paper strips. Remove it from the mould by cutting it into two sections, then join the two sections back together. For detailed instructions on working with moulds, see pages 40 and 44-45, Steps 1 and 2.

3 Make a base for each animal from glued paper strips. Dry thoroughly. Model the flowers for the rabbit ring from tiny paper strips. Leave to dry as before.

△ *A rabbit with good table manners.*

Modelling napkin rings

Mark the tube every 1³/₈in (3.5cm) and cut it into rings at the marks. Mix the wallpaper paste to full strength. Coat the strips and apply them smoothly round the card ring. Leave rings to dry in a warm place, then add another layer of paste. Dry rings thoroughly.

Decorating the rings

1 Stick each animal on to a ring and paint with a base colour. Using the pictures as a guide, decorate the rings as described in previous chapters. Paint the small details last. Protect the paint with two coats of varnish.

2 Cut the ears for the sheep and cow in two layers of different coloured felt. Stick the shapes together and fold the cow's ears in half as shown. Use clear glue to stick them in place. Add ribbon trims as desired.

▷ *A speckled rooster is a favourite farmyard animal and this one makes an appealing subject for a papier mâché napkin ring.*

Pattern shapes for animal napkin rings

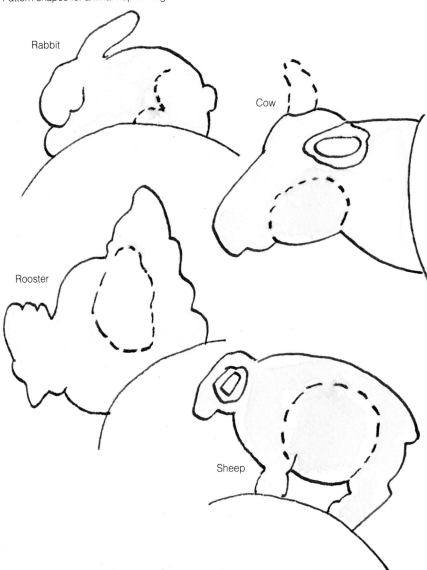

Rabbit

Cow

Rooster

Sheep

Folding paper napkins

*Napkins folded into intricate designs are a quick
and stylish way to decorate your table settings. Origami is the
Japanese name given to the art of paper folding
and all the effects shown here are achieved with a few simple folds.
With practice, you can create crisp designs in minutes.*

For an effective display choose good quality, firm paper napkins, at least 15in (38cm) square.

Plain coloured napkins can be extremely effective; strong colours will show off your designs to their best advantage. If you want to create a more vibrant look, try experimenting with different patterns and designs.

Stripes work particularly well on geometric designs such as the fan fold, while a simple border enhances designs in glasses.

A strong visual effect can be created by buying two sets of 2-ply napkins in contrasting colours or tonal shades. Split them and then join the two different halves. A variation on this is to buy two different sized napkins so that once rejoined, a border is created — particularly effective if you use one plain and one patterned napkin.

The fan fold is a simple and effective way of presenting paper table napkins. Use florals for prettiness, or stripes for a bold statement, and choose colours to co-ordinate with the table linen and crockery.

Making a fan fold

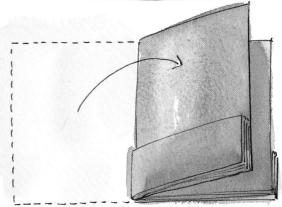

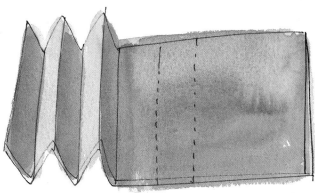

1 Fold the napkin in half. Starting at one end, pleat two-thirds of the napkin widthways into a series of 1in (2.5cm) pleats.

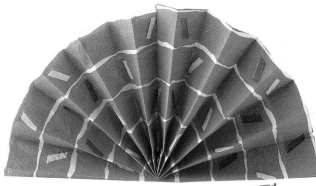

2 Fold the pleated napkin carefully in half, making sure that the edges meet and that the pleated section is situated on the outside.

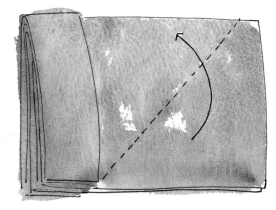

3 Hold the napkin with the folded edge at the top then fold up corner A, so that it overlaps the first top fold.

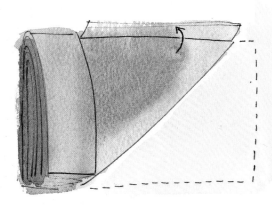

4 Neatly fold the overlapping piece down over the top folded edge and behind the triangular section of the napkin.

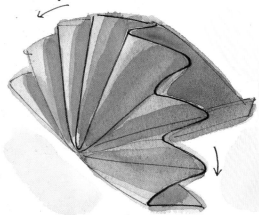

5 Place the folded overlap and base of the pleats on the table. Open out the pleats to form a fan.

◆ TIP USING A GLASS

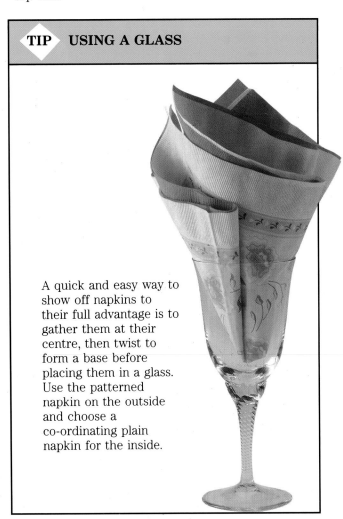

A quick and easy way to show off napkins to their full advantage is to gather them at their centre, then twist to form a base before placing them in a glass. Use the patterned napkin on the outside and choose a co-ordinating plain napkin for the inside.

Card storage boxes

*Attractive large scale storage boxes
are hard to find. The solution is to make your own from thick
card, then cover them with wallpapers chosen
in colours and textures to complement your decor. Add toning
cords and ties as subtle finishing touches.*

Decorative storage boxes can take pride of place stacked on the tops of cupboards and chests, or be put to work as good looking and practical space fillers inside cupboards or even under beds.

The three boxes pictured in this section are all designed to be seen together. Each is covered in a 'natural' fibre-effect wallpaper, with the coarsest texture used for the large box and the smoothest, silkiest finish for the smallest. The handles and ties are made by twisting together lengths of colour-blended haberdashery cords, tapes and twine. Protective corners cut from leather-effect, sticky-backed plastic add a practical and decorative touch.

▽ *Fabric-look wallpapers in natural shades and subtle textures are ideal for covering storage boxes.*

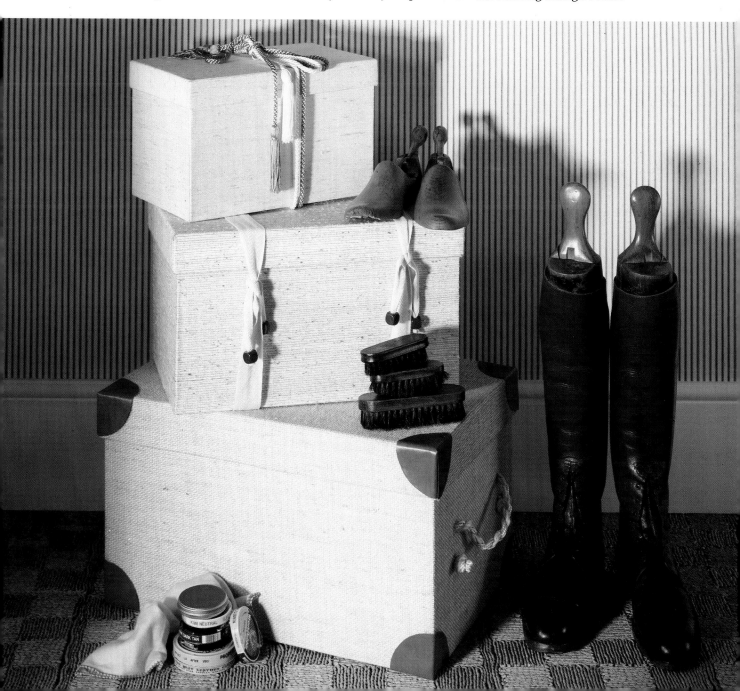

Materials and equipment

Card to make the boxes should be strong enough not to sag but thin enough to cut without difficulty. Sheets of mounting card (mat or Bristol board) or Pasteline board (mechanical or illustration board), available from artist's and graphic suppliers are ideal weights to use. Between one and two sheets are needed for each box, depending on the size of box required.

Papers to cover the boxes should be wide enough to cover the lid and each side without a join. Wallpapers are a good choice, as they can be used straight from the roll, so a box can be 'wrapped' round, with one single seam. The boxes can be lined with matching or contrast papers — wallpapers are perfect for this too.

Adhesives Use a suitable glue for each job. Stick the card with clear multipurpose craft glue. Use masking tape or gummed brown tape to reinforce the card folds and joins. Spray adhesive suitable for mounting photographs can be used for sticking the wallpaper to the boxes. This is quick and easy to use but surrounding areas must be protected with newspapers. Alternatively use a PVA glue (white glue) spread evenly and thinly across the back of the paper. Use clear craft glue or PVA adhesive (white glue) for sticking down any stubborn edges and corners on the papers.

Cords and ties for handles and fastenings can be made from a variety of materials. Dressing gown cords with tassels make luxurious looking ties, while matt and silky cords twisted with garden twine make robust handles on large storage boxes. Braids can be used as handles or straps, fastened with simple knots, tied as bows, or threaded through buckles or D rings.

Other materials needed are a ruler and a straight (preferably metal) edge to cut against, a protective surface for cutting card (a craft cutting mat is ideal), set square, pencil, eraser, sharp scissors, a strong craft knife, stiletto (awl) or hole punch and sticky-backed plastic for making corner protectors.

Making a basic box

Each of the boxes shown in this section is made in the same way. The basic box is made from four separate side pieces and a base section. The lid, which is made from a single sheet of card, is cut out after the box has been assembled. This is to make allowance for the thickness of the box sides and to ensure the lid does not fit too tightly.

1 Decide on the size of box required and, with a ruler and set square, draw the base rectangle on card, placing the shape on the card as economically as possible. Cut out with a craft knife against the straight edge of a metal ruler, pressing on to a protective work surface.

2 Mark out and cut two box sides to the same length as the base and as tall as required. Cut out.

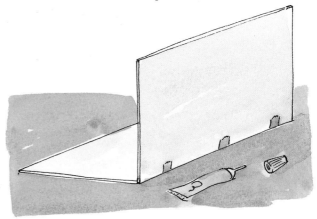

3 Run a line of adhesive along one long edge of the box base and butt one side piece against this at right angles. Hold side to stick it in place and anchor with small pieces of masking tape. Repeat with other side section.

4 Measure the outside width across the base of the box, to include the thickness of the card and cut out two end pieces, to same height as side pieces. Run a line of glue along the side and base edges of one end of the box and press an end piece in place. Secure the end with pieces of tape. Repeat at other end of box.

5 When the glue is dry, stick masking tape along each join on the outside of the box, extending it by 1in (2.5cm) at top and turning this to the inside. Stick tape along the inside joins too.

To make the lid

1 Measure across the outside width and depth of the box and note the measurements. Adding ³/₈in (1cm) to each measurement, draw a rectangle to this size on a sheet of card. Extend the lines and mark out the depth of the lid. Between 1¹/₂in (4cm) and 2¹/₂in (6.5cm) is a good depth, depending on required box size.

2 Cut out round lid shape, then gently score along lid outline. Bend card into lid shape. Run a line of glue along the side edges and press to stick. Hold each corner in place with a piece of masking tape, then secure with longer strips, as for the basic box, when the glue is dry.

Covering the box

The instructions given here are for covering a box with wallpaper, which can be wrapped round the box in one length. Other smaller size papers should be cut to fit round in four sections; two with side overlaps at both ends of the longest sides of the box and two for the short sides, cut to fit the width exactly.

1 Unroll the wallpaper and lay the box on its side on the wrong side of the paper, at right angles to the edge. Wrap the paper round the box, and cut, leaving sufficient to make a 1¹/₂in (4cm) overlap. Trim the depth of the paper, so that there is an overlap at the top of between 3in (7.5cm) and 5in (12.5cm) and an overlap at the base of between 2in (5cm) and 3in (7.5cm). (Adjust these sizes as desired to fit your box)

2 Spread adhesive over one long side of the box, or spray with adhesive. Lay paper along glued box side, aligning side overlap so it reaches over to the short side of the box. Run a line of adhesive down back of overlap and press in place. If the paper is heavily textured, neaten the overlap with a strip of masking tape.

3 Work round the box, glueing each side in turn and pressing the paper flat. When overlap is reached, glue along back edge of paper and press it over the overlap, so that cut paper edge is level with the corner of the box. Trim the edge if necessary.

4 Lay the box on its side and make a straight cut at each corner, up to the base of the box. Fold the flaps over to the base and mitre each corner. To do this draw a straight line diagonally from corner to corner, across the folded flaps and trim the paper along these lines. Glue the overlaps flat.

5 Cover the base with a rectangle of paper cut ¹/₂in (1.2cm) smaller all round than the box base. Stick in place with adhesive spread evenly over the surface.

6 Lay the box on its side and at each corner cut straight down to the card edge. Spread adhesive on the backs of each overlap flap and smooth them down on to the box inside. Thick papers can be trimmed at a slight angle at each end, so they fit neatly into the corners.

Covering the lid

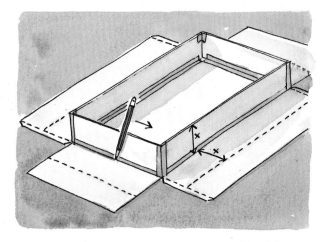

1 Lay the lid upside down on the wrong side of the paper, and draw round outline. Remove lid. Extend the drawn lines at the corners to the depth of the lid sides and mark these lines. Draw these proportions again, to allow for the paper to reach up inside to the lid top. Mark in $^3/_8$in (1cm) side overlaps on each end of the longest lid sides as shown.

2 Cover the lid top evenly with adhesive and lay it on to the paper, matching outlines. Spread adhesive on the backs of longest side pieces and overlaps and press in position. At edge of lid, snip overlaps so they fit neatly over the edges. Glue backs of short overlaps and press in place.

Lining the box

1 To line the lid, cut a paper rectangle large enough to fit inside the lid and to overlap the edges of the top cover paper very slightly. Stick the lining in place.

2 To line box sides, measure their width and depth. Linings should cover top paper overlaps by about 1in (2.5cm). Cut two long side linings with slight overlaps at each side and base, and two for short sides with overlaps at base edge only. Stick long linings in place first, then short ones. Push linings well into the corners. Cut a rectangle to fit the base.

Different handles and ties

Twisted cord handles

These handles are ideal for larger boxes as they are strong — being made from a number of cords twisted together. Make each handle by securing the ends of three or four different cords and strings with sticky tape. Allow plenty of cord as the twists and knotted ends reduce their length. Twist the cords together evenly and secure ends with tape.

Mark the handle position on outside of box and pierce two holes from the inside, just large enough to take cords. Pierce two more holes about 2in (5cm) below these. Knot one end of the twisted handle and push through to the inside. Thread up and back through to the outside. Push back through to the inside and pull tight. Thread handle out through lower hole. Ease handle back to adjust twists. Decide on finished handles size, then knot ends. Cut off the taped ends.

Tape ties

These are made by securing tape through slits in box base and neatening ends with wooden beads. Measure width of box base and lightly mark a quarter of this measurement in from each side. Measure 2in (5cm) in from each long edge and mark. Measure the width of the tape and use a craft knife to slit a line to this size along marked positions on box base. Cut two tape lengths to fit round box and tie easily. Thread each through to inside, then out of box. Squeeze tape ends through wooden beads and secure with glue.

Cord and tassel ties

Dressing gown cords in toning colours can be simply wrapped and tied round a plain box, or they can be secured to the base of the box in a chosen position with a little craft glue. Spread adhesive along the centre part of each cord and stick in place.

Protective corners

Make protective corners from circles of paper covered with sticky-backed plastic.

1 Measure depth of lid and set a compass to this measurement. Draw eight circles on cartridge weight paper and cut out.

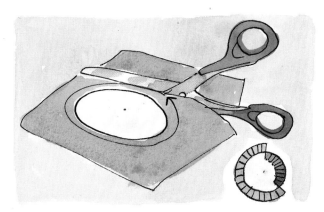

2 Peel backing from plastic, cut a little larger than each circle and stick to circles. Cut round $^1/_2$in (1.2cm) from edge. Make snips up to paper all round. Fold each overlap to wrong side, taking care that circle edge is smooth.

3 Cut straight up to the centre point of patch. Fold one cut edge in slightly and glue flat. Fold circle over box corner. Align so the neatened edge is overlapping and level with the box edge. Glue in place on box corner.

Découpage 1

*Découpage is the traditional craft of sticking paper
motifs to objects and then applying layers of varnish for a
lacquer-like finish. By choosing the shapes and patterns
you use carefully and cutting and arranging them with style, you
can turn even the most ordinary item into something special.*

Découpage is a French word which means 'cutting up'. The craft became popular in Europe during the seventeenth and eighteenth centuries, and was inspired by the elaborately decorated and expensive lacquered furniture imported from China and Japan. This budget-conscious alternative was widely regarded as a cheap way of producing decorated furniture for a wider market, although some pieces, especially those from Italian craftsmen, were particularly fine in their own right. The Victorians rediscovered découpage, and made it into a fashionable pastime, saving their Valentine cards, magazine cuttings and using books of printed motifs to decorate screens, boxes, table tops and other small objects.

△ *There are no rules about what to découpage —
here a tray has been given a new lease of life with the
addition of appropriate motifs. Attractive and unusual
labels from bottles of liqueurs transform what was a
simple tray into an elegant drinks server. The varnish
gives a hardwearing finish.*

Themes and sources

Although favourite subjects for découpage have always
been fruit and flowers, birds and butterflies, themes
can also be suggested by interests and hobbies —
keen cooks might enjoy designs based on food pictures
or recipes, while gardeners have a wealth of material
in their catalogues and seed packets.

Holidays, with the souvenirs of tickets, postcards
and photos, make good themes too, as do historical
events, famous people and animals.

Wallpapers, old books, children's story books and
damaged prints are good sources for découpage subject matter, so it is worth browsing through antique
fairs and junk shops for 'finds'. Victorian style decals
— those paper shapes designed for use in scrap books
and découpage — can still be found too.

Surfaces for découpage

Wooden objects are traditionally used as a base for
découpage, but other surfaces may also be suitable.
Whatever you choose must be firm and strong enough
to take the dampening effect of pasted paper and the
weight of many coats of varnish. The aim is to build up
a surface which is perfectly smooth and shiny, so that
it is impossible to feel the outline of the paper cut-
outs beneath the varnish.

As a beginner, it is best to start with a small project
such as a box, picture frame or tray base. Plain unvarnished wood boxes and other flat surfaced items
suitable for découpage can be bought from specialist
craft suppliers. But objects that have lost their former
glory are also good subjects to decorate and disguise
under cut-outs and varnish.

Materials and equipment
Paper motifs

Well-drawn images are best for cutting out, so look for
motifs with a clear outline. The paper shapes used
should be of equal thickness and must be able to withstand the effects of paste and varnish. For this reason
magazine pages may be unsuitable as the paper can
disintegrate during the découpage process.

Avoid papers with printing on both sides, as the
image may show through. It is worth experimenting,
however, with a favourite cutting; some papers are
more resilient and can be treated with an acrylic sealer
spray, available from artist's supply shops.

Thick papers, such as greetings cards, can be
thinned down to make them more manageable. Wet
the back of the card with a damp sponge until the card
is soft enough for a paper layer to be peeled away.

Thin papers, which would allow the varnish to seep
through, can be strengthened by sticking them on to
thicker paper. The image is cut out when dry.

Suitable objects

Almost any item can be used, but trays, boxes or picture frames are ideal for the beginner. These can be
made of wood, metal, glass or plastics. To provide a
good base, make sure that the surface is thoroughly
stripped of any flaking paint or old varnish before you
start. Bare wooden surfaces must be sealed before
starting to apply the motifs.

◁ *Wood may be the traditional choice of surface for
découpage, but there is no reason why this functional
metal watering can cannot be used as well.*

Tin tray

Wooden boxes

Craft glue

Wallpaper paste

Craft roller

Découpage motifs

Découpage papers

Craft knife

Clear paste wax

Varnish

Scissors

Tweezers

Sealer

Paint brushes

Wire wool

Sanding block

Glasspaper

Abrasives

You will need a sanding block and a medium grade glasspaper (sandpaper) to rub down the surfaces to be decorated. A fine grade glasspaper, fine grade wet and dry paper and 000 grade wire wool (steel wool) will be used for subsequent sanding processes.

Paint

If some of the surface is going to be left uncovered and you want to paint it, use a water-based vinyl primer (primer/sealer) and oil-based paint for wood, or the appropriate paint to suit the base material.

Varnish

Between ten and 20 coats of varnish should be used to build up a deep and smooth finish. Choose either a clear satin finish interior varnish or an interior tinted varnish.

Brushes

You will need three ½in (1.2cm) or smaller brushes for applying the paint, glue and varnish.

You will also need: manicure scissors or a scalpel (X-acto knife) for cutting out the paper shapes, wallpaper paste or transparent craft glue for sticking down the paper cutouts (you may find that a craft roller will help press the shapes in place) and clear or white paste wax to buff the final surface.

Preparing the surface

Use a sanding block and some medium grade glasspaper to rub down the surface area of the object you are about to découpage. Make sure that no flaky paint or old varnish remains, and pay particular attention to any corners.

Wipe the dust away with a lint free cloth, and then coat the surface with paint or varnish. If you are using paint, follow the manufacturer's instructions and apply enough coats to give a good, smooth surface. Leave the object to dry for at least six hours, then lightly rub over the surface with fine glasspaper.

Cutting out paper shapes

Follow the step-by-step instructions below to cut out a selection of paper motifs. Use a pair of manicure scissors or, when cutting around intricate shapes, use a scalpel. Cut out more shapes than you will need to allow choice when assembling the design.

1 Thinly drawn lines on a motif may need thickening. Use a pencil or marker (not water soluble) to draw a firm outline. This will make cutting out easier. Choose a colour to match the design.

2 Delicate shapes like fine flower stems may need strengthening to prevent them from tearing. Make bridges by drawing sections between two areas of the design. These can be cut away once the pattern has been glued to the box.

3 Cut around the design, leaving a narrow border of paper around the drawn outline. This makes it easier when cutting away interior shapes. To cut them, pierce a hole with the tip of the scissors, insert them from below and cut around the outline.

4 Cut around the outside edge of the pattern holding the scissors at a slight angle so that the paper has a bevelled edge. This thinning of the outline helps the paper blend with the background.

Découpage 2

*Armed with a selection of paper cut-outs, now
learn how to glue them in place and apply the coats of varnish.
Your aim is to achieve a satin-smooth surface with a deep
sheen, then the paper design you have created will take on a
warm glow and an antique quality.*

Applying the paper motifs to a prepared surface does not take long, but it is worthwhile spending a little time beforehand experimenting with different layouts.

The cut-outs can be applied to form a picture or composition that grows over the shape of the object, allowing some background surface to show through, or they can be built up to cover the entire object with a rich kaleidoscope of colour. Place large shapes under smaller ones and overlap some of the designs to vary the effect. Use tweezers to handle fragile shapes.

The varnishing process, however, does take some time. Between ten and 20 coats of varnish should be used to build up a deep and smooth finish. The varnish should be left overnight to dry thoroughly between coats, so a project will probably take at least two weeks.

The work should be left undisturbed as much as possible and kept away from household dust or steam. A small project can be worked on an old tray so that it can be put away while drying.

Gluing the cut-outs

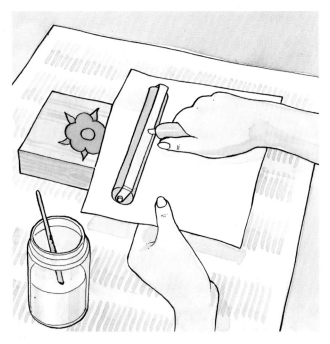

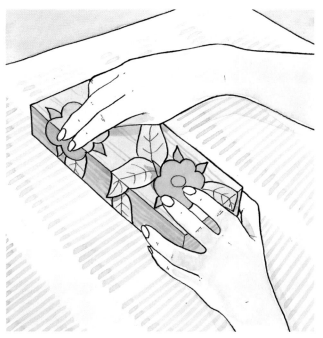

1 Before you start, protect the work top with old newspapers. Then, starting with the largest shapes, spread glue evenly across the backs of the paper cut-outs and press gently in place. Use a piece of plain, thick paper to protect the pattern while you press the shape in place with a craft or wallpaper seam roller or gentle hand pressure.

2 Continue adding the paper shapes in this way, leaving the edges of overlapping shapes unstuck so that patterns can be slipped underneath. If the object you are covering has angles, such as the corners of a box, arrange the cut-outs so they reach over the edges. This is to prevent the paper from lifting after it has been varnished.

Applying the varnish

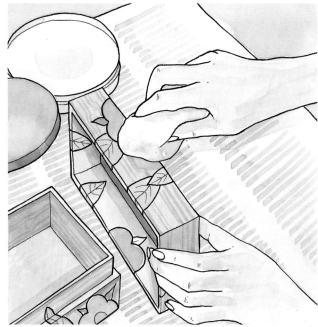

1 When the shapes are firmly stuck down and dry, apply a coat of clear or tinted varnish, brushing in one direction. Use the varnish sparingly, then leave to dry. Clean the brush with white spirit after each use. When the varnish has dried, rub it gently with fine grade glasspaper and wipe the dust away. Repeat the varnishing and rubbing down process, wet-sanding the surface after every third coat.

2 Continue varnishing and sanding until there are between ten and 20 layers of varnish, alternating the direction of the brushstrokes between each layer. The edges of the paper cut-outs should be undetectable to the touch below the layers of varnish. Finally, rub the surface over very gently with fine wire wool, then polish the surface with white wax, using a soft cloth.

DESIGN IDEAS

Lazy découpage

If the idea of découpage appeals, but the thought of spending such a lot of time on a single project does not, then here are some 'mock' découpage alternatives. Lazily based on the real craft, the aim is to go for quick cover-ups and fun finishes or even something a little more off-beat.

△ *If you are tired of the same old lamp base, why not give it a totally new look? Glue torn-up pieces of newspaper on to the base until it is completely covered. Finish with a few coats of varnish.*

◁ *Keen gardeners can use seed packets to brighten up a dull corner of their potting shed. Here, the packet fronts have been glued on to drawers. Paint on a few layers of varnish to protect against wear and tear.*

▽ *This useful stationery box has been decorated simply with used stamps. Varnish will add protection.*

Playing card box

This size box is an ideal starter project for trying your hand at découpage. You can buy unvarnished wood boxes to use as a base, but any suitably sized box or tin could be used. The colour of the box and the paper shapes have been carefully chosen to coordinate with the design on the playing cards.

You will need
◇ Box or tin in required size
◇ Vinyl paint in colour to blend with papers (alkyd or acrylic for wood, enamel for tin)
◇ Paper cut-outs
◇ Medium and fine glasspaper (sandpaper)
◇ Sanding block
◇ Three ½in (12mm) or smaller brushes for applying paint, glue and varnish
◇ Turpentine to clean varnish brush
◇ Wallpaper paste or transparent craft glue
◇ Sharp pointed scissors, manicure scissors, scalpel (X-acto knife) and tweezers
◇ Clear satin finish interior quality varnish
◇ 000 grade wire wool (steel wool)
◇ Clear or white wax
◇ Lining material such as sticky-back plastic velour, otherwise use découpage, thick paper or felt

To make the box
Prepare the box by removing any decorative catches and hinges if possible, then sand and paint the box as described on pages 25-28. Arrange the

cut-outs so the design 'grows' over the surface. Complete the découpage process and replace the fittings. The box is now ready for lining.

Lining the box
Sticky-backed plastic with a velvet finish is easy to use for lining a box, and well suited for its use here. Measure the inside of the box, and cut lining pieces to fit each side, allowing an extra ¼in (6mm) for overlaps at the sides on two of the opposite sections, and ¼in (6mm) along the base line on all side sections. Cut a piece to fit the base exactly. Repeat this sequence to line the lid.

Stick the linings in place, starting with the two sides with overlaps, followed by the two other sides, and then the base. Finally, push each piece well into the corners, to ensure a good fit.

Colored foil découpage

*Scraps of coloured foil can be arranged under
glass to create lustrous découpage designs. Assemble a
kaleidoscope of simple shapes like spots,
squares or rectangles, and use them as unusual decorations
on plates, vases or picture frames.*

Sweet and chocolate wrappings, available in a wide variety of colours, textures and designs are an ideal material for working this style of découpage.

Glass dishes, bowls and vases with smooth or textured surfaces can be decorated with foil découp-age, provided the containers have openings wide enough to allow a hand inside. As foils tend to be more fragile than other papers, use simple-to-handle geometric shapes, and use the finished piece for decorative, rather than practical purposes.

△ *This delicate, foil-lined vase is purely decorative. A smaller bowl, inside the vase, holds the flowers.*

Materials and equipment

Foils For best results choose clean undamaged foils, smoothed flat before use. Discard pieces with small nicks or flaws, as the paint used to give a protective backing layer to the découpage could seep through and spoil the effect.

Cutting tools A sharp craft knife or scalpel (X-acto knife) and a straight edge to cut against are needed for cutting foil squares and rectangles. A wad punch and selection of fittings (available by post from craft suppliers) is useful for cutting accurate circles. A protective work surface is also needed.

Adhesives As foils are not porous, they will prevent even clear-drying craft adhesives from drying out completely, so use a spray adhesive (available from art supply shops) which leaves a fine sticky film on the surface of the foil .

Paint Choose a metallic-finish paint suitable for glass and ceramics, or a coloured enamel paint.

Other materials needed are tweezers, scissors, solvent for paint and adhesives, tissues, a watercolour brush and old newspapers to protect the work surface from adhesive spray and paint splashes.

Working foil découpage

1 The glass must be clean and dry on both sides. Cut out a selection of foil shapes, taking care not to damage the edges. Add foreground and small shapes first. To test placement of foil shapes for the design, put glass so right side faces you and gently hold foil on damp fingertip or with tweezers to wrong side of glass.

2 When you have enough foreground shapes, lightly spray adhesive on the wrong side of the glass in the appropriate area. Gently drop the foils in place and press flat. Leave to dry slightly, then gently remove excess sticky mist from surrounding areas with a solvent-dampened tissue. Lay a sheet of clean paper over design and press gently to flatten.

3 Continue adding shapes, overlapping edges slightly and removing excess adhesive from glass as you work. The design can be a small motif or an all-over design. If the latter, do not work quite to the edge of the glass, but leave a small area so the backing paint can overlap the foil edge. When the design is complete, check all shapes are flat and secure, and spray back with an even covering of adhesive. Gently press larger pieces of foil over this for extra protection. Leave to dry.

4 Brush a layer of paint over the back of the foil, covering the edges neatly. Continue painting over the rest of the glass if desired. Leave to dry, then repeat with second coat of paint.

△ *This colourful grid design is emphasized by the mottled texture of the chunky glass ash tray.*

△ *No need to paint the back of these foil strips — the backing card will protect the design on this frame.*

△ *An exuberant mix of punched foil spots and random squares adds sparkle to a plain glass dish.*

Lasting pleasures

Paper flowers in all shapes, sizes and colours
can be as vivacious and colourful as tropical blooms or as
delicate and pale as spring blossom. Whether
you choose to copy nature or create larger-than-life fantasies,
paper flowers will provide an everlasting display.

The art of paper flowers

Paper flowers have a timeless appeal all their own. They are an attractive alternative to fresh or dried flowers and give you the freedom to re-create the simplest or most complex of Nature's designs throughout the year.

The skill of creating realistic displays with paper lies in the fashioning of small details; this will soon come with practice. It is worth taking time to examine real flowers, or realistic pictures, so you can reproduce the structure in paper and wire. As paper flowers require little outlay in the way of materials or equipment, they are also an inexpensive option for brightening a room.

The basic techniques

Although paper flowers can be made in a variety of ways, all the methods involve the placing of cut-out petals around a central stem. The technique will depend on the type of flower you are making and the template you use to do this. Petals can be cut as individual shapes, a single circular flower shape or as a long continuous strip of petals.

This section shows you how to use crêpe paper with single petal templates to create timeless poppies and anemones. Other flowers you can make using this method are tulips and roses.

Materials and equipment

Crêpe paper is available in two thicknesses, single and double. Double crêpe paper provides extra rigidity when curling, stretching and moulding flowers and leaves.

Specialist equipment
All the equipment needed is available from florist's suppliers.
Florist's wire is a fine flexible wire used to secure leaves and petals in place.
Wire stems are stronger than florist's wire and do the same job.
Gutta tape is a green sticky tape used to bind stems, anchor petals and disguise joins.
Cotton balls can be bought ready made and are fixed to the central stem to make the flower centre. You can also use balls of paper.

◁ *These colourful anemones are quick and easy to make.*

Anemones

Bring a splash of colour into your home with a brilliant and everlasting bouquet of paper anemones. Simple and bright, they add the perfect finishing touch to any room. Templates for the stamens, leaf and petal are given overleaf.

You will need
◇ Crêpe paper; yellow, violet, pale green, deep rose, black and white
◇ Gutta tape (floral tape)
◇ Cotton balls
◇ Black paint or black felt tip pen
◇ 11in (28cm) wire flower stems
◇ Fine gauge florist's wire
◇ Scissors and small pliers
◇ Clear contact adhesive
◇ Pastel crayons (optional)

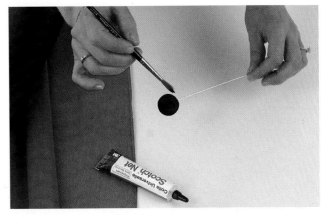

1 With the pliers, bend over the end of a wire stem and push it into a cotton ball. Secure with adhesive. Paint the cotton ball central boss black, or colour with felt tip pen.

4 Position each of the petals around the central boss and stamens. Carefully arrange them in two rows of three, with each of the petals slightly overlapping.

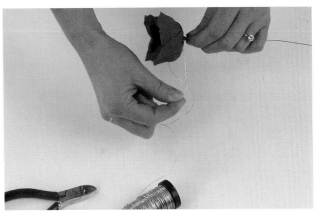

5 Firmly bind the petals to the stem with a length of florist's wire. A dab of adhesive at the base of each petal will help hold them in place as you work.

Poppies

These dramatic, bright red poppies are made in almost the same way as the anemones. Each flower is made up of 15 petals, rather than six and the centres are slightly more complex. The leaves are made from two sheets of crêpe paper and strengthened with wire. You will find templates overleaf.

You will need
◇ Crêpe paper; red, black
◇ Gutta tape (floral tape)
◇ 1¼in (3cm) cotton balls
◇ 12in (30cm) wire flower stems
◇ Fine gauge florist's wire
◇ Adhesive
◇ Black and green paint or felt-tip pen

To make a flower centre

Fix a wire stem into a cotton ball, as before. Paint the ball green then use black paint or a felt-tip pen to draw the centre markings.

Arranging the petals

Arrange as before, building up four or five rows of overlapping petals.

To make the leaves

Using the pattern, cut out two shapes for each leaf required (each stem has two leaves). Place a piece of wire between them, 1in (2.5cm) from the base, and glue the two leaves together. Attach the leaves to the stems with wire and gutta tape as shown for the anemones.

2 Using the pattern, cut out the anemone stamens from black crêpe paper. Cut the fringe and run a line of adhesive along the opposite edge. Position around the central boss and stem.

3 Carefully cut out six petals in the colour of your choice, using the pattern. Gently ease and stretch each petal inwards in order to create a realistic curve.

6 Starting at the base of the petals, wind the gutta tape around and down the stem. Keeping the tape taut, continue until all the wire is covered, easing out any creases as you go.

7 Cut out three leaves from the green crêpe paper using the pattern. Fix them to the stem with wire and cover the joins with gutta tape. Fine details (leaf veins) can be added using a pastel crayon.

Poppy leaf

Poppy petal

Anemone leaf

Anemone petal

TEMPLATES

To cut out your templates, trace the petal and leaf patterns on to stiff card. Carefully cut out each shape then place them on your crêpe paper. Draw around the outline with a soft pencil and cut out, repeating as often as necessary.

Poppy stamens — 14in (35cm) long

Anemone stamens — 8in (20cm) long

Papier mâché bowls

*Highlight the beauty of unusual and semi-sheer
tissue papers in eggshell-thin, papier mâché bowls. Made with
thin layers of paper, the bowls are both quick
to do and pleasing to look at and, as they are shaped over an
existing bowl, they can be made to any size.*

The technique used to make these bowls is a clever way of displaying the beauty of unusual handmade and fine papers. The bowls are made by the conventional paper strip method, but instead of building up many layers of paper, the number is reduced to give a translucent effect which is enhanced by using coloured tissue mixed with other thin papers.

The colours of the paper can be chosen for their own beauty, or to co-ordinate with the decor of a room. The rim of the bowl is left deliberately ragged to emphasize the delicacy of the layers. While these bowls are very appealing, they are not sturdy and can only be used for decorative purposes.

Materials and equipment

Bowl Use a bowl with gently rounded sides and base and no lip as a mould for the papier mâché. If you use a plastic bowl do not let it get too hot during the drying process in case it melts.

Tissue paper Select a variety of colours that complement one another. Tear them into strips. A few dark tones will help to create interesting patterns.

Paints Any paints can be used, such as watercolours, enamel or spray paints, or paints for use on glass and ceramics. Metallic paints give a particularly attractive lustre.

Other materials are a large jar or tin can, petroleum jelly, PVA glue (white glue), non-fungicidal wallpaper paste, paint brushes, scissors and clear polyurethane varnish.

Making the bowl

1 Mix up the wallpaper paste to a fairly thick consistency. Leave to stand so it becomes thicker. Mix in some PVA glue to strengthen the paste.

2 Cover the outside of the bowl with a thick layer of petroleum jelly. Turn bowl upside down and rest it on a jar or tin, so that it does not touch the work surface. Wrap a layer of paper strips around it, using water as a binding agent. Do not use glue on the first layer otherwise it will be difficult to remove the papier mâché from mould later.

3 Once the initial layer of paper has been applied, begin to use the paste, brushing it over the paper strips. Begin to build up a design, by using different papers of your choice. Do not worry about keeping the rim neat.

4 Apply about three layers of paper strips, continually smoothing them down with the brush to avoid air bubbles or lumps of glue developing. Then leave the bowl overnight in a warm place to dry out thoroughly — in an airing cupboard or near to a radiator, for instance but not on a direct heat source.

5 When the papier mâché is dry, ease it off the mould to check that it is dry. Re-grease the mould and replace the papier mâché bowl. Add more layers of different coloured papers to create a pattern. Choose dark colours for a striking effect. Light colours will produce a more subtle design. When the layers are finished, leave the bowl to dry again.

6 Ease the papier mâché off the mould, taking care not to damage the ruffled edge.

▽ *Eggshell-thin papier mâché — made with just a few well-chosen layers of paper — has a very different quality to the traditional style, which uses many layers. The type of paper used is very important as it will be on display and, as shown with these examples, it forms the primary decoration. The bowls below are also enhanced with spatters of gold paint — particularly noticeable with the bowl on the left.*

7 Decorate the inside of the bowl with pasted strips — tissue is most effective — arranged as desired. Leave to dry again. At this stage you may wish to brush on some extra colour with a paint brush. Alternatively, you could spatter the paint by drawing a blunt knife towards you across the brush.

8 Coat the bowl with about three layers of varnish, allowing each layer to dry before adding the next. Varnish helps to keep the bowl rigid and protects it as well, by making it more waterproof.

DESIGN IDEAS

◁ *Use the paper graphically to create striking patterns. Tissue paper is an ideal choice — when it is layered, a third colour or interesting shadow is formed.*

▷ *Introduce extra texture to the papier mâché by sandwiching wisps of silky thread between the layers of paper. The lines formed by the thread contrast well with the more solid areas of the paper.*

▽ *Plan the choice of colours in advance, then build up the pattern with touches of paint — fine lines or spatters of a strong colour add interest.*

Papier mâché masks

*Masks have been used for centuries
to fascinate and intrigue, concealing their wearers' identity.
Papier mâché is simple to use and can be
shaped and decorated in so many highly effective ways
that it is a natural choice for mask making.*

From Carnival and Mardi Gras to fancy dress parties, the·atmosphere of celebration, magic and mystery has always been enhanced by the wearing of masks. These can range from simple cut-out shapes used to disguise the face, to highly decorated and elaborate creations designed as dramatic focal points in an entertainment.

Making masks

Masks are usually shaped over a mould or armature. Papier mâché, which is both light to wear and inexpensive, is an ideal material to work with. In this section we show you how to make a plasticine mould, shape papier mâché strips over this, and decorate the finished mask in a variety of different ways.

Design ideas

Tragedy and comedy are immortalized by masks; the familiar down-turned mouth epitomizes sadness, the upturned smile laughter — these are symbols of the theatre. The stark white Pierrot's mask is a familiar image, and one that is easy to recreate. For inspiration, decoration and exotic ideas, look at books on Africa, the Far East or Venice, as masks feature largely in their traditional celebrations. Carved wooden masks used in ritual dances, Chinese dragon masks, and the sophisticated and mysterious gold and silver masks associated with Venetian carnivals can all be used as starting points for your own masks.

Materials and equipment

Apart from materials such as the papers, glues, paints and varnish mentioned on page 43, other items required are:

A work board, like a pastry board, or other practical work surface that is easy to clean.

Plasticine is available in 1lb (500g) packs. Four of these packs should be sufficient to make a life-sized mask. The plasticine can be re-used.

Modelling tools and a **kitchen knife** are used to shape the plasticine.

Petroleum jelly is used to grease the surface of the plasticine, to prevent the papier mâché from sticking to the mould.

Sandpaper for smoothing the surface of the papier mâché mask before it is decorated.

Paint brushes, both fine artist's

Moulding the plasticine

If the mask is to be lifelike, persuade someone to act as a model for you. Otherwise use a mirror, or photos as a guide.

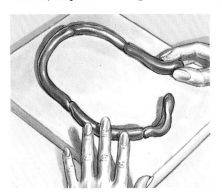

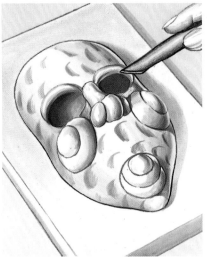

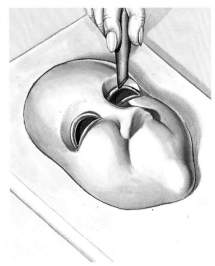

1 On the work surface, knead the plasticine to warm it, then work some into rolls and lay these out to make the outline of a face. Fill in the shape with lumps of plasticine, gradually building them up to make a flattened mound, like a face without the features.

2 Using a knife and modelling tool sculpt the plasticine to create a brow line, eye sockets and the shaping of cheeks and chin. Add small lumps of plasticine to build up the cheek areas, and the nose.

3 Position the eyes on the mask so the wearer will be able to see through them. Make the eyelids from small rolls of plasticine and blend into the face with the modelling tool. Hollow out the eyeball area, so the papier mâché can be smoothed over.

Painting and decorating

By using materials and colours in an imaginative way it is possible to create quite fantastic effects. All the trimmings and details used to decorate the masks featured on page 43 were added when the masks were painted and varnished.

Before adding any glued-on decoration, make sure the surface texture is evenly coloured. If the trimmings are to be spray painted, (see our exotic fern-trimmed mask) these details can be coloured before attaching them: a quick spray of paint on the completed mask will unify the finished effect. Use fine artist's brushes to draw details.

Three dimensional decorations can be added in different ways.

Inserting decorations

This method of inserting decorations is ideal for adding materials which have stems, such as pieces of plastic foliage, wired flowers and leaves or feathers.

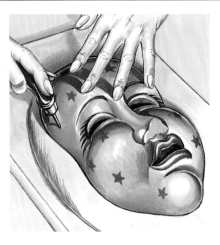

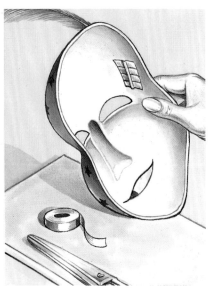

1 Pierce the mask in the appropriate position using a bradawl or large sewing needle. The size will depend on the diameter of the stem which should fit tightly. Insert the decoration and turn the mask to the wrong side.

2 Spread superglue on the protruding stem and press it to the back of the mask. Continue adding details in this way.

3 Secure and neaten the stems on the back of the mask with paper strips or brown paper tape. Either cut separate strips to cover each stem or, if the stems are close together, cut a large strip to cover all the stems. Stick in place with craft glue.

brushes for adding features and other details, and flat-edged bristle brushes for larger areas, and to varnish the finished mask.

Beads, sequins, feathers and other trims are needed to decorate the masks. Plastic flowers and foliage are ideal for exotic effects, and can be sprayed with paint. Flower stem wires are good for making whiskers on animal masks. Make a collection of useful materials to keep at hand.

Spray paints such as metallic paints and car spray colours are ideal to use as they dry quickly.

Clear superglue is the best type of adhesive for sticking most decorations to the masks, but craft glue can be used for sticking fabric and paper details.

Paper tape like brown sticky tape is used to neaten the mask inside.

Thin card is used to make details.

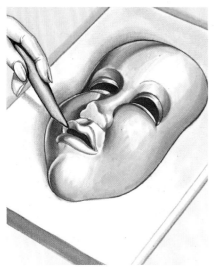

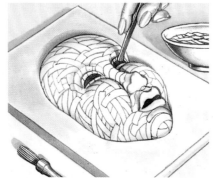

Working the papier mâché

The glue and paper strips are prepared and used as described on page 40. Use small paper strips on intricate areas.

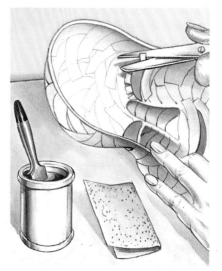

4 Model the lips from rolls of plasticine and join these to the face. To create an open mouth, hollow out the space between the lips in the same way as the eyes.

1 Smear a layer of petroleum jelly over the surface of the plasticine and work the papier mâché over the mould. Build up at least six layers of paper strips. Use the modelling tool to shape the papier mâché into the eye sockets, and smooth over the surface.

2 When the mask is complete leave it to dry in a warm place, then ease it from the plasticine mould. Trim the edges if necessary and smooth the surface with sandpaper. Snip away the excess paper inside the eye and mouth shapes. Paint with undercoat.

Attaching card shapes

Details like ears, and other extensions can be cut from card, decorated as you wish, then stuck to the mask by means of a hinge flap.

A variation is to join the card shape to the mask by dividing the hinge flap so the central part of it slots through the mask. The rest of the hinge is glued to the surface.

1 Draw the shape on to card and add a hinge, about ½in (12mm) deep. Crease the card along the hinge fold line. Cut out and paint the shape.

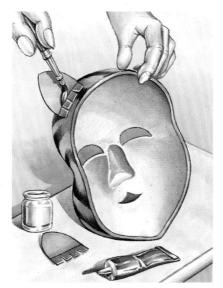

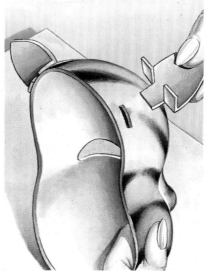

2 Make two or more snips in the hinge up to the fold line, so that the card can be curved to shape if necessary. Spread glue under the flap, and press the card on to the mask. Disguise the join with a dab of paint, or other decoration.

3 For extra stability the card hinge can be partially inserted. Make the card shape then snip the hinge flap to make a central flap. Make a slit in the mask and slot the flap through. Glue to the inside of the mask. Stick and colour the surface mounted flaps as before.

Surface joined details

Flower stem wires are a good choice for making animal whiskers. These and other details like small feathers or flower stems can be attached to the mask with paper strips. These can then be painted to camouflage the join.

Details such as lace and netting can be stretched across or secured to the masks with glue. Other details can be added on top of these.

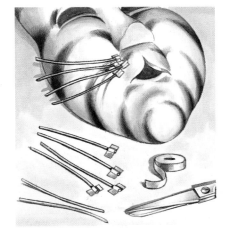

1 Cut the whiskers to size, then cut strips from paper or sticky paper tape and lay over the wire ends. Glue the strips, and press the whiskers in position. Disguise the strips by colouring over them.

2 To make a lace or net veil or cap, cut the fabric to size, and dab a little superglue along the edges. Press the fabric on to the mask. Glue on a braid or beaded trim to hide the raw edges.

Wearing a mask

Masks can be worn by securing them to the face with tapes or elastic attached to the sides of the mask and held behind the head. Alternatively, fix a stick under the jaw line of the mask which can then be held up to the face.

To attach tapes or elastic, stick the ends in place with superglue, or hold them with staples.

To insert a stick pierce a hole and push in a length of flower cane. Anchor it behind the mask with tape or glued paper strips.

DESIGN IDEAS

△ *An exotic Venetian carnival mask with intricate painted designs.*

▽ *Netting in brilliant yellows and oranges adds mystery and colour.*

◁ *A sophisticated carnival mask with a head piece of satin and gold fabric hung with decorative beads and tassels.*

▽ *A highly-decorated mask sports gilded leaves, beads, net, lace and a dramatic ruched collar.*

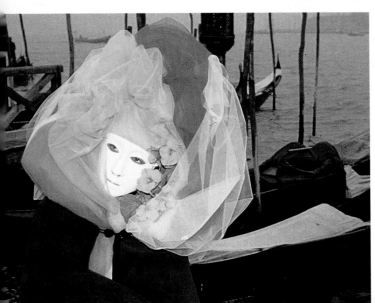

Pierced paper lace

*Use old lace and embroidery designs as inspiration
to create a collection of intricately decorated papers for
stationery, pretty borders and trims. The relief
texture is worked along a drawn outline by piercing rows of tiny
holes with a sharp point.*

Making pierced paper lace is a leisurely activity; the simple technique of pricking out a design dictates its own unhurried rhythm. Traditional lace patterns and embroidery transfers make ideal starting points for your designs, as they are easy to copy and their linear nature adapts well to paper.

Paper lace effects

The pattern motifs can be used singly as monograms or repeated to form bands of pattern. These can be used in many imaginative ways, from edgings on personalized notepaper and decorations on greetings cards to more ambitious home furnishing projects like picture mounts and paper blinds.

To work the designs, the paper is first laid on a padded surface. The motifs are then pricked through with a needle or another sharp tool. The size of the holes can be varied to emphasize certain areas of the design, and the paper can be pricked from both sides to produce a texture of smooth and raised holes. This contrast gives depth to the finished designs.

Materials and equipment

Design motifs to copy and use as inspiration. Choose simple designs with clearly drawn outlines.

Papers used for making pierced paper lace should be smooth and fairly stiff, to support the closely spaced holes. If the paper is thin, repeated piercing will weaken sections of the design and cause it to split. Matt and shiny writing papers are ideal and so is canson paper and other art papers. Try out effects on a variety of papers before making a final choice of your chosen designs.

Sharp points to prick out the lace design can be a selection of different size sewing needles. The size

of the hole depends on the thickness of the needle. Alternatively, use a stiletto (awl) or book binding stabber. These have a sharp point set into a handle.

Polyester wadding or **thick felt** to cover the work surface. The padding should be smooth and even so that the needle point reaches to the same depth each time it pierces the paper.

You will also need: HB pencil, eraser, fine black fibre tip pen, tracing paper, sharp scissors for cutting around outlines and low-tack adhesive tape for holding tracings in place.

Transferring designs

To transfer the design it must first be traced as accurately as possible. The tracing is then transferred to the paper — the design should be marked clearly at this stage so that it is easy to follow when the paper is pierced. However, try to use only very light pencil strokes which can be erased later on when the work is complete.

One of the best ways of transferring a tracing is to place it over a light source such as a window so that the design shows up more clearly when a sheet of paper is placed over it. The design can then be re-traced on to the top paper.

1 Take a tracing of the required design motif, and reinforce the outlines with fine black fibre tip pen. Tape the tracing to a window, and position the paper over it. Hold securely with tape and softly trace off the design. To repeat a motif, simply remove the top paper, re-position and trace again.

2 Another method is to reinforce the tracing in black as before, and tape it to a glass-topped table. Position the paper over the tracing and place one or two small table lamps (shades removed) under the table. Re-draw the design.

Working the design

The smooth and raised holes are worked from both sides of the paper. The holes can run parallel to each other to make outlines or can be arranged in contrasting groups. To work raised holes as separate motifs within a design, trace the complete design on to both sides of the paper before you begin.

1 Put the paper, right side up, on the padded work surface. Holes pierced from the right side will have smooth edges. Decide which part of the design is to have this treatment and start working along the appropriate outlines.

2 Use light pressure and even wrist movements to pierce the rows of holes. Space them evenly, leaving the width of a hole between each row to avoid splitting the paper.

3 To work raised holes on the right side of the paper the design must be pierced from the wrong side. Turn the paper over and use the existing pin holes as a guide to working the design.

△ Border designs can be used to edge shelves or decorate blinds. This design has raised hole flowers and leaves picked out with softly contrasting smooth holes.

Different effects

Piercing paper with a sharp point produces a finely detailed pattern. For a less formal effect with a coarser texture, experiment with implements that will produce much larger holes, such as a hole puncher. Fold the paper like a concertina so that the pattern will be repeated through the layers.

▷ Different point sizes can be combined in one design to add subtle changes of texture.

◁ Mount a beautiful example of paper lace in a pretty frame and give it pride of place with other treasures.

TIP	STITCHES

The decorative stitches on a sewing machine can be used to create rows of small repeating designs. Practice stitching designs through layers of typing paper. Use machine embroidery thread to create coloured effects. Experiment with different sized needles. Use twin needles to duplicate designs side by side.

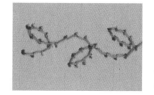

△ Pierce wallpaper borders for a prettier, lacy effect

CHAPTER II
PERSONALIZE WITH PAPER

◇

◇

Paper beads

*Although paper may seem a rather fragile
material to use, it is ideal for making a wide range of hardwearing
and extremely attractive jewellery. Here strips
of paper have been used to create a unique range of beads that are
both stylish and inexpensive.*

Working with paper

Strips of paper, cut or torn from larger sheets, can be used to create beads in a wide range of shapes and styles. You can use single sheets of paper or glue (laminate) thin pieces of paper together. It is a good idea to use layers of laminated paper in place of thick paper or card, as it is stronger and far more flexible.

If you are laminating paper, it is important to remember that whichever of the sheets of paper you put the paste on will expand and contract more than the other, resulting in a curve. This happens when identical papers are joined, and even more noticeably when different kinds of paper are laminated. You will also find that the final effect often depends on how you cut or tear the strips. It is worth experimenting, as different types of paper will tear in different ways.

Using paint

There are numerous effects that can be achieved using paint. Plain colours in a variety of finishes such as matt, gloss or metallic can look extremely elegant. Alternatively, you could try applying a base coat, then paint or spray splashes of a contrasting or toning colour on top. For the more adventurous, simple paint effects such as marbling (see pages 89-92) can be used. These special effects can be worked on the paper before rolling, or on the finished beads.

If you are using pale colours, you will achieve the best results with white paper. Bright metallics work particularly well on darker colours, and two-tone pastel or natural colour effects are both extremely effective.

Making paper beads

By tightly rolling up strips of paper you can create a variety of attractive looking beads, which can be made into necklaces, bracelets, earrings or used to decorate hair ornaments. Large-scale beads can be made from very long strips, cut from a length of wallpaper. Use these to make chunky jewellery, or combine them with small beads on a home furnishing project, such as a bead curtain.

For added protection, coat the finished beads with clear varnish or nail polish before threading them on to cotton, silk, leather or wool strands.

You will need
- ◇ Paper
- ◇ Knitting needles in different sizes, straight skewers or cocktail sticks
- ◇ Scissors or craft knife and metal cutting edge
- ◇ Petroleum jelly
- ◇ Wallpaper paste or adhesive stick
- ◇ Artist's paint brush
- ◇ Paint (optional)
- ◇ Clear varnish (optional)
- ◇ Plasticine

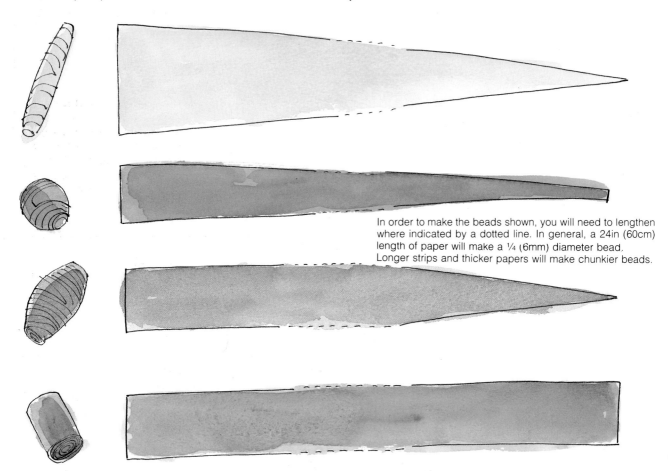

In order to make the beads shown, you will need to lengthen where indicated by a dotted line. In general, a 24in (60cm) length of paper will make a ¼ (6mm) diameter bead. Longer strips and thicker papers will make chunkier beads.

1 Mark out each bead strip on your chosen paper using a ruler and pencil (the more accurate you are at this stage the more uniform each bead will be).

Use the shape ideas given here and experiment with different dimensions to create larger or smaller beads. Cut out each of the bead strips.

Using decorative paper

Using coloured or patterned paper removes the need for painting. Try paper that has a special finish, such as waxed or metallic paper (available from stationers and specialist shops). Alternatively, look out for wrapping paper and magazine pages with unusual designs and colour combinations.

For an attractive two-colour effect, cut two strips of paper in different colours for each bead and trim one so that it is narrower than the first. When rolled together, stripes are produced.

Loosely curled beads

These create a striking three-dimensional effect, and are made by gluing together two contrasting strips of tapered paper. While the glue is still wet the paper is curled round a knitting needle or piece of wood dowelling, and held in place with a rubber band until the glue has dried.

Torn paper beads

Subtly coloured beads that look like pottery can be made from several shades of soft artist's paper. Tear a strip in the base colour to measure roughly 3½in (9cm) long and 2½in (6.5cm) wide. Tear a strip in a second colour to the same length, but a little narrower. Tear a third strip narrower still, and a little shorter than the second strip. Coat each strip on either side with wallpaper paste, and place them one on top of another. With the narrowest strip on the outside, roll them together over a large knitting needle. Use rubber bands to hold the layers loosely until dry, then coat with a thin layer of varnish.

Layers of colour will show all around the bead (see below).

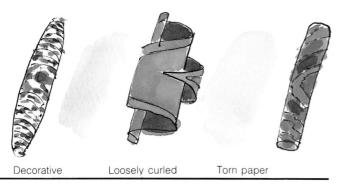

Decorative   Loosely curled   Torn paper

2 Cover a knitting needle, skewer or cocktail stick with petroleum jelly. Coat one side of the paper strip with a thin layer of wallpaper paste or glue using an adhesive stick.

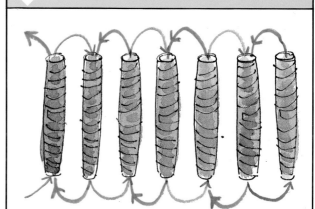

◆ TIP   MAKING A BRACELET

Thread straight sided beads with hat or shirring elastic to make attractive chokers and bracelets.

To make a bracelet, measure your wrist and line up sufficient beads to fit, plus one or two extra. Working with the elastic still on its card or spool, thread the beads, leaving a long end of elastic. Arrange them side by side and work back through the beads in the opposite direction. Join the two end beads, stretch the elastic, knot the ends and push them down into one of the beads.

3 Starting at one end (this will be the wider end if you are using a tapered strip of paper) roll the strip tightly and evenly around the knitting needle. Make sure the end is secure by adding a little more glue if necessary.

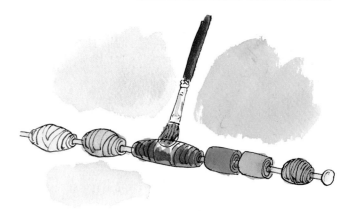

4 Remove the bead and leave to dry. Repeat with the remaining strips. When painting or varnishing the beads, you will find it easier if you thread them on to a knitting needle first. Leave the beads to dry by embedding one end of the needle in plasticine.

DESIGN IDEAS

Here are just a few ways in which paper can be
used imaginatively to make a variety of stylish
beads. Layers of torn paper, pages from
magazines, gift wrapping
and plain paper — the
choice is endless.

Pleated paper jewellery

*Paper is not an obvious material
to choose for making jewellery — but it is surprisingly strong
and extremely versatile. Paper can be layered, gathered,
threaded, punched and squeezed in a variety of innovative ways
to make unusual and eye catching designs.*

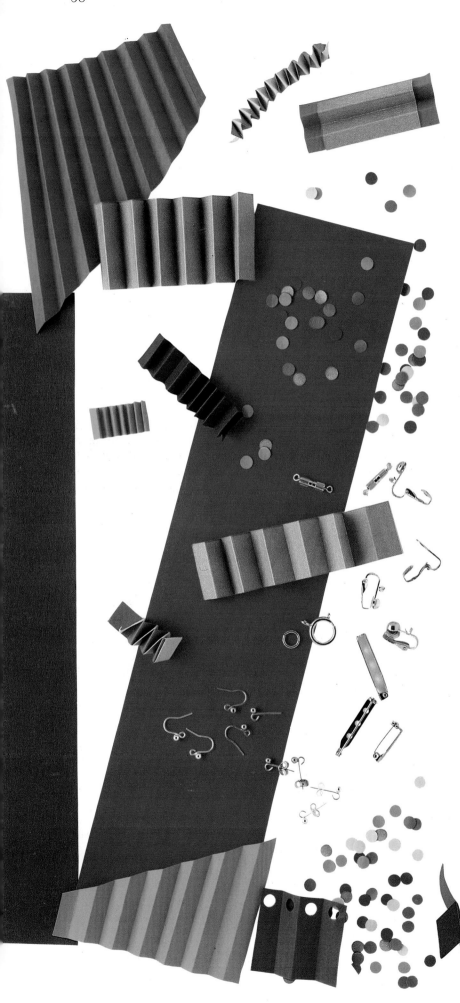

Paper jewellery

You know paper jewellery looks good when people express surprise at the material! It has a lovely spur of the moment appeal, and is ideal for accessorizing holiday or other lightweight clothes. Pleated paper is particularly suited to jewellery making because the pleating adds rigidity. The pleats can be held in place with glue, or secured with rolled paper beads, (see page 54 for instructions on how to make these) and ribbons and cords.

Choosing papers

Brightly coloured papers are a natural choice for jewellery making, and firm closely textured artist's papers are ideal for pleating. Choose papers that do not curl or mark easily. Thin papers can be used if they are doubled over or pleated with a thicker paper which will give support. Try out different effects before starting a design, to see whether the paper handles well and to experiment with colour schemes. The finished jewellery can be given extra durability by spraying with an acrylic fixative or a varnish suitable for paper.

Materials and equipment

Papers in a selection of colours.
Jewellery findings are the attachments — the clips, studs and pins used for making jewellery. These can be bought from craft shops and mail order suppliers.
A craft knife and **metal ruler** are used for marking pleats and measuring and cutting the paper.
A paper punch gives a professional finish to threaded pleats. Use a punch with a single hole cutter, preferably with a removable base, as this type is easier to position, or use a belt hole punch.
Adhesives for sticking the pleats together can be stick adhesive, or a PVA adhesive (white glue). Transparent super glue is used to stick the findings to the finished jewellery.
You will also need a pencil, eraser, scissors, set square, compass, matching ribbons and cords, and a surface to cut against.

Pleating variations

By varying the width of the pleats, quite different effects are achieved. Narrow ¼in (6mm) pleats give a delicate effect, suitable for earrings and small details. Larger pleats, up to ½in (1cm) wide give a bolder effect, particularly when folded double to make rigid ruffles. Use these for hair ornaments, neck bands or bracelets.

Concertina pleats can be laid one over the other in graded lengths, and cut with curved or straight edges. They can be fanned out, or secured as knife edge folds.

Cross-over pleats are made from two strips of paper laid at right angles across each other to form a stretchy chain. These can be given sophisticated treatments with interesting colour variations.

Cutting concertina pleats

To prevent the pleats from twisting or lying unevenly they should all be the same size, and folded accurately and parallel to each other. Pleated bands which will lie over one another should all be made with equal width pleats, otherwise they will not overlap properly; the pleats should fit into one another exactly. Remember when cutting out paper ready for pleating, the paper size will be dramatically reduced after pleating, so cut a longer length than you think you will need.

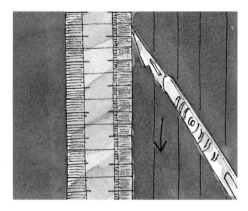 

1 Mark out each pleat fold line with a craft knife, scoring lightly against the edge of the ruler. Use the scored side as the wrong side of your work.

2 With the wrong side of work facing, fold the first pleat back towards the wrong side. Make the last pleat fold the same way to give a neat edge shape.

Layering pleats

Many different effects can be achieved by varying the width and shapes of the different layers.

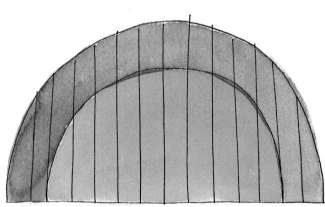 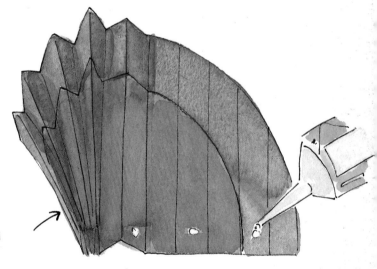

1 To make a curved edge, cut two half circles, one slightly smaller than the other, and fold each with equally sized pleats. Lay the smaller shape over the larger one, positioning it centrally and, with straight edges level, pinch the pleats together.

2 Treating the layers as one, secure the pleats by adding a tiny spot of adhesive between each pleat. If the pleats are to be held by a paper bead, this is not necessary; simply dab a little adhesive to the outside edges, and push into position.

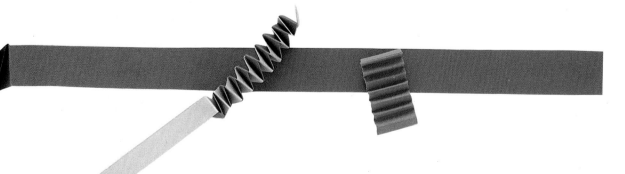

Triangle shapes can be pleated and layed across one another to form bows, or cut in half to make interesting fan shapes that can be fitted into beads and used as earrings or brooches.

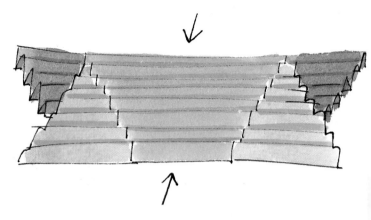

3 Cut three triangles in three different sizes and colours. Pleat each triangle, pleats running parallel to the base line, and lay them over one another, smallest triangle on top.

4 Gather up the layers at the centre to see the effect, and trim the points of the triangles to balance the shape if necessary. Squeeze the pleats together at the centre, and finish design as desired.

Cross-over pleats

These can be made from any width of paper strip, but all strips pleated together should be of equal width.

1 Hold two strips at right angles to each other, and fold the strips over and over each other, taking care to keep the fold lines straight. This ensures the finished strip will keep in shape.

2 To add a new strip, simply fold the strips together until the paper runs out, then taking note of the fold positions, unfold the strips slightly, and trim the end to the last fold line. Stick the new strip in position over the end, lining up the new end with the crease line. The ends of the pleated chain are joined this way, to make a band.

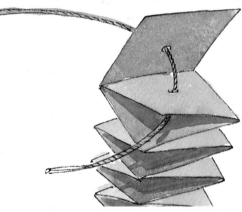

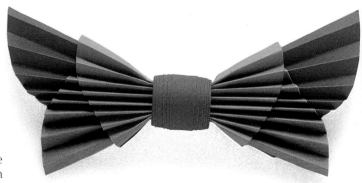

3 To thread cord through a chain, make a small hole through the two end folds. Wrap the cord end with sticky tape, and thread through. Remove tape and glue cord end behind pleat. Stick the two end folds together to cover the cord and strengthen the chain.

Papier mâché jewellery

Seaside shapes and colours are combined in a
coordinating necklace and bangle set. The jewellery is made using
two different methods; papier mâché pulp is moulded
to shape the bangles, and layers of laminated paper are built up
to form the necklace motifs.

Papier mâché jewellery is inexpensive and lightweight — an ideal extra for your holiday wardrobe.

By using ready-made materials such as plastic bangles as moulds for the pulp, and compressed paper balls for the necklace, a complete set of matching jewellery is quick and easy to create.

Design ideas

Simple shapes and bold colours work best for papier mâché jewellery. Use the slight unevenness of the material to advantage when adding decorations. Stripes and spots and splashes of colour applied with quick brush strokes give a childlike spontaneity to the designs. Copy the designs featured here, or use the techniques to develop your own decorating ideas.

Papier mâché pulp

This is made from scraps of torn up paper. When gauging amounts remember that paper reduces considerably as it softens. The scraps are added to water and boiled to a pulp, which is then sieved and mixed with paste. Next it is hand moulded over a base shape which is left inside the finished papier mâché to act as a support while the mixture dries.

Materials and equipment

Newspapers and bathroom tissue for the pulp.
A large saucepan is required for boiling the pulp.
A bucket and stick are used for holding and stirring the pulp.
A food blender can break down the boiled paper.
A large sieve is used to strain the wet pulp.
Wallpaper paste; any cellulose paste without fungicide can be used to make the papier mâché.
Plaster of Paris; a small quantity added to the pulp will help speed the hardening process.
Fine sandpaper is used to smooth the papier mâché surface before painting, and to give a 'key' to surfaces used as a base for the papier mâché.
Paints like poster paints or acrylics are ideal for decorating the finished designs.
Clear varnish suitable for paper or interior use will protect and provide a waterproof finish.
Paintbrushes; use medium size and fine water colour brushes to paint the designs, and a medium size brush to apply wallpaper paste and varnish.

2 Tip the mixture into a bucket and stir it until the texture is even, or run the mix a little at a time through a food blender. Strain the pulp through a sieve, and press it down well to remove as much water as possible. If the pulp is too wet it will slip on the mould and take a long time to dry.

3 Make up the wallpaper paste to full strength following the manufacturer's instructions. Stir the paste a little at a time into the drained pulp. Avoid over-wetting the mixture, which should remain fairly stiff. Sprinkle in some plaster of Paris, and stir thoroughly. The pulp is now ready for use.

Papier mâché bangles

Make up your own designs or copy our bangles decorated in simple stripes.

You will need
◇ Prepared papier mâché pulp
◇ Two plastic bangles
◇ Poster or acrylic paint
◇ Clear varnish
◇ Paint brushes

1 Tear the papers into very small pieces and place in a saucepan with a little water. Bring to the boil, then let the mixture cool.

1 Rub each bangle inside and out with sandpaper to roughen the surface. This provides a grip for the pulp. Squeeze and smooth the pulp a little at a time over each bangle. Make sure that you apply it thinly to the inside edges so that your hand can still pass easily through the bangle.

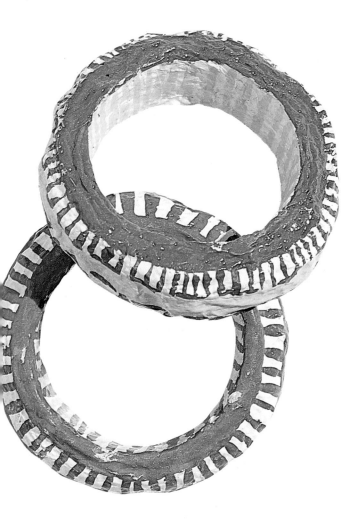

△ *These papier mâché bangles have a fashionable primitive look, reminiscent of tribal art designs.*

2 Leave the bangles to dry completely in a warm, well ventilated position. This process can take up to twenty-four hours. Rub lightly over the surface with sandpaper to even out any lumps and bumps.

3 To paint each bangle, hold between fingers and thumb and brush over with white paint. To avoid smudging the work, paint a small area at a time and leave it to dry before progressing. Work the yellow patterns next, followed by the blue stripes. When completely dry, varnish the bangle inside and out.

Papier mâché motifs

Flat motifs are made from layers of torn paper sandwiched with wallpaper paste. When it is dry, designs are cut out and decorated.

Materials

Paper for the pulp and a **paste brush.**
Vaseline — smear a thin coat over the work surface to prevent the paper sticking to it.
Craft knife or **scalpel** for cutting out the shapes.
Thick needle or **bradawl** for piercing holes.

1 Tear the papers into pieces roughly 6in (15cm) square. Place one layer of overlapping pieces on the greased work surface and paint over them with wallpaper paste. Apply another layer of torn paper to the pasted surface and add another coat of paste. Smooth the surface with your hands, pressing it flat to remove any air bubbles. Continue in this manner until the 'sandwich' is about ¼in (6mm) thick. Leave to dry completely before lifting.

2 Place papier mâché on a clean protective surface and trace or draw patterns on to the papier mâché. Use a craft knife to cut out the shapes. Start by pushing the blade into the angles of the design, and cut away from these. Smooth the cut edges with sandpaper, and pierce holes for threading. The motifs are now ready to paint.

Papier mâché necklace

You will need

◇ Prepared papier mâché layers
◇ Twenty-four ¾in (20mm) diameter compressed paper balls
◇ Shirring or round hat elastic

◇ Thick needle or bradawl
◇ Knitting needles
◇ Paints, brushes, varnish, thick needle and craft knife as for bangles and motifs

1 Make up seven motifs as described, using the picture as a guide. Paint them with a white base coat and leave to dry completely. Decorate with the yellow and blue patterns.

2 Before painting the paper balls, first pierce each one through the centre and thread them, six at a time, on to thin knitting needles. Paint the balls white, and leave to dry completely by balancing the needles in jars or across two objects. Paint the stripes and patterns, copying our picture.

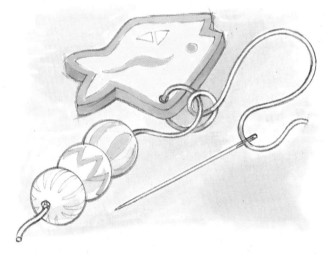

3 To thread the necklace, take a length of elastic, (double the length if using shirring elastic). Thread this through three or four beads, then thread through a motif. Twist the elastic into a knot, then thread the elastic through more beads. Pick up another motif, and continue threading in this way, arranging motifs closer together if desired. Knot the elastic ends together, and ease knot back through beads to conceal join.

Desk top stationery

*Paper-covered desk sets make covetable
accessories as well as ideal gifts. Choose from mix and match
patterns or smart plains and geometrics.
The inspiring variety of paper enables you to choose design
themes to suit any style or colour scheme.*

Desk top stationery sets can look sleek and functional, pretty and feminine, or even rather grand — it is the choice of paper that creates the effect. The stylish desk set pictured here — comprising a letter rack, notepad cover, blotter pad, pencil pot and paper-clip box — is covered with chintz-patterned papers, which blend equally well in a home, office or the work corner of a sitting room.

All the designs are simple to make using giftwrap papers and cardboard. We chose four different but complementary papers to create a subtle pattern mix. Try copying this idea to suit your own colour scheme, or use one giftwrap paper to co-ordinate your desk set.

Materials and equipment

Papers Use easy-to-fold medium-weight paper. Patterned giftwrap gives professional results as the designs help to camouflage and neaten overlaps and corners. Some wallpapers and art papers are also suitable. Line the stationery with contrasting plain or textured paper.
Card should be strong enough to hold its shape. Artists' mounting card and display board are good weights. Card cylinders with bases and box lids make useful small containers for clips and pins.
Adhesives Use spray adhesive to stick paper to card (make a spray booth from a large carton), and clear craft glue, masking tape and gummed paper tape for assembly.
Other materials required are a craft knife, scissors, ruler and set square, straight edge to cut against and protective work surface.

Letter rack

Try to position the covering giftwrap so that the pattern matches up on each tier.

You will need
Materials already listed including:
◇ One sheet mounting card (mat board or Bristol board)
◇ Three sheets giftwrap paper

1 From card cut a rectangle for the base 9 x 4³/₈in (23 x 11cm) and a 9in (23cm) square for the rack back. Cut a rectangle 10 x 5in (25cm x 12.5cm) from giftwrap, and spray the back with adhesive. Place base card centrally on sticky paper; trim excess away.

2 Cut a 10in (25cm) square of giftwrap and spray with adhesive. Stick rack back centrally on this and trim excess, leaving ³/₈in (1cm) on top edge. Press the excess over the card.

3 With the covered side of the card facing upwards, run a line of glue along the side of one long edge of the base. Stand the rack back, covered side facing forwards against the base. Press to stick. Hold in place with masking tape until dry.

4 Cut a card rectangle 9 x 3¹/₈in (23 x 8cm) for the front and a rectangle of giftwrap 10 x 4in (25 x 10cm). Spray giftwrap with adhesive and position front card centrally. Trim, leaving ³/₈in (1cm) on top edge. Press excess over card.

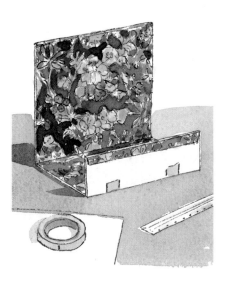

5 Run glue along the remaining long edge of the base. Stand the front against the glued edge with the covered side facing the rack back as shown in the diagram. Press to stick. Hold in place with masking tape until dry.

Notepad cover

The notepad cover is designed to fit average-sized notepads measuring about 5³/₄ x 4in (14.5 x 10cm). If you are making a cover for a larger or smaller notepad, simply adapt the measurements of your materials.

You will need
Materials already listed including:
◇ One sheet giftwrap
◇ One sheet leatherette paper
◇ 6in (15cm) length petersham
◇ Notepad about 5³/₄ x 4in (14.5 x 10cm)

1 Cut two card rectangles 6³/₄ x 5¹/₄in (17 x 13cm) for covers and a card strip 5¹/₄ x ³/₄in (13 x 2cm) for the spine. From giftwrap cut a rectangle 15³/₄ x 6¹/₂in (39.5 x 16.5cm). Place card pieces on wrong side of giftwrap, as shown, and mark their positions on the paper.

◁ *Covered with chintz-patterned giftwrap, an ordinary notepad becomes a stylish desk accessory.*

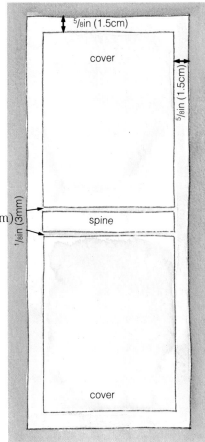

⁵/₈in (1.5cm)

cover

⁵/₈in (1.5cm)

¹/₈in (3mm)

spine

cover

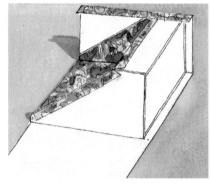

7 Run glue along the side edges of the rack back and along the short edges of the base and front. Position the side pieces as shown. Reinforce joints with gummed tape.

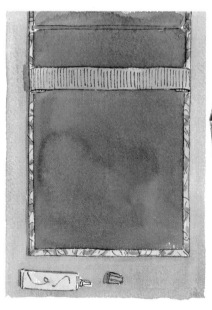

8 Cut a rectangle of giftwrap 19¼ x 9⅝in (49 x 24cm). Spray with adhesive. Matching the centre

of the paper and the rack back, and with top edges level, smooth the paper round the rack. To trim excess from sides and front, lay rack on its sides and trim carefully. Cut a strip of giftwrap to fit front width with ³⁄₈in (1cm) overlap at base. Spray with adhesive and stick in place.

9 To make back divider measure out a card rectangle 5½in (14cm) high to fit across rack width, plus ⅝in (1.5cm) at each side for glue tabs. Cut out. Measure and cut a shorter divider 4in (10cm) high, as wide as the back divider. Score and bend tabs.

10 Cut giftwrap to fit divider fronts, allowing an extra ³⁄₈in (61cm) at tops and sides. Spray and cover card. Fold excess to wrong sides. Cut two more pieces of giftwrap to fit backs exactly and stick in place. Glue along tabs and stick inside rack, matching marked lines. Cut a piece of giftwrap to fit base. Trim to ⅛in (3mm) less than base all round; spray and stick giftwrap in place.

6 Cut the sides from card as shown. Cut two rectangles from giftwrap 10 x 5in (25 x 12.5cm) and spray with adhesive. Place side card pieces centrally, and trim excess, leaving ³⁄₈in (1cm) on the slanted and short upper edge. Snip to corners and press excess over edge. Trim away the extending giftwrap. Mark the divider positions with pencil, as shown.

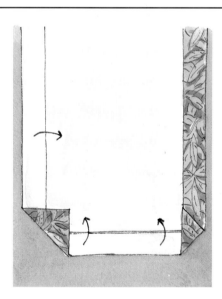

2 Remove card and spray giftwrap with adhesive. Replace card in positions marked. Fold the corners of the giftwrap over the card, then the side edges.

3 For the lining, cut a rectangle of leatherette paper measuring 13½ x 4¾in (34 x 12cm). Spray with adhesive and press in position on to the cover back.

4 To make the strip to hold pad, fold in one end of petersham for ½in (1.2cm) and glue to inside of cover, 1½in (4cm) below spine. Fold other end to match, trimming if necessary, and stick in place. Alternatively, attach petersham with decorative stud or eyelet. Slip notepad through petersham.

TIP SURFACES

To protect the finished stationery set against scuffs and dust, spray with acrylic sealer (available from art shops). Then coat with varnish for a glossy look.

Blotter

You will need

Materials listed, including:
◇ Thick card for backing board and thinner card for corners of blotter
◇ Two sheets giftwrap
◇ One sheet leatherette paper
◇ Blotting paper

1 For backing, cut card rectangle 19½ x 13½in (49.5 x 34cm). Cut giftwrap cover, allowing 1in (2.5cm) extra all round for turnings. Spray and cover board, folding corners and side pieces as for notepad.

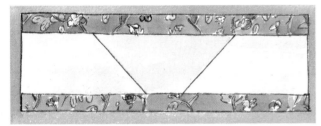

2 To make the blotter corners, cut four right-angled triangles with angled sides measuring 4in (10cm) from thin card. Cut four strips 8 x 4in (20 x 10cm) from giftwrap. Spray backs with adhesive and press triangles on top. Fold edges over as shown.

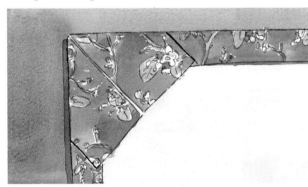

3 With wrong side of backing card facing, slip the corner pieces under each corner and fold ends over card. Glue ends firmly.

4 Cut a rectangle from leatherette to line blotter back, cutting paper ¼in (6mm) less all round than blotter size. Stick in place with spray adhesive.

Pencil pot

You will need

Materials listed, including:
◇ Cylindrical container with metal base
◇ One sheet giftwrap
◇ One sheet leatherette paper
◇ Compass

1 Trim container height to 4in (10cm). Cut a rectangle from giftwrap to wrap round container, allowing ⅜in (1cm) overlap at top and sides.

2 Spray giftwrap with adhesive. Wrap round pot, aligning lower edge of paper with pot base. Snip upper overlap level with pot top; press to inside.

3 Cut a rectangle of leatherette paper to fit inside pot, ¼in (6mm) shorter than inside height, plus a small overlap at side. Spray with adhesive and coil loosely, sticky side outwards. Place inside pot, align with base, then carefully smooth against sides.

4 Cut out a circle of lining paper the same size as pot top. Spray with adhesive and stick inside pot.

Paper-clip box

You will need

Materials already listed including:
◇ Small box lid
◇ One sheet giftwrap
◇ One sheet leatherette paper

1 Cut strip of giftwrap long enough to wrap round box sides, allowing an extra ⅝in (1.5cm) overlap at side, top and base. Spray with adhesive and wrap round box. Snip to corners; press to inside and base.

2 Cut leatherette paper strip for lining, ¼in (6mm) narrower than box height. Spray with adhesive. Coil loosely, sticky side outside. Press into box.

3 To line inside and outside base, measure inside box top; cut two leatherette paper pieces to fit. Spray and press into position.

Covering books

*Worn books, folders and photo albums
can be given a new lease of life with covers made from
a variety of materials and papers.
With a little flair these and everyday stationery can be
transformed into stylish keepsakes.*

Tired-looking book covers, whether on indispensable address and recipe books or favourite collections of photos, can be recovered with the minimum of outlay. Simple wrap-over paper covers are familiar to all who have brightened up well-thumbed school books, and this technique can be taken a little further to produce covers worthy of designer stationery shops.

Old and new covers

Existing bookcovers, providing they are not badly damaged, can be covered with paper or a mixture of paper and fabric, sticky-backed plastic or even leather and suede. The insides of the covers are then faced with end papers which join the cover to the pages and are thick enough to camouflage the cover turnings. End papers are made with a single sheet at each end of the book which is glued inside the cover and across the first (or last) page.

Completely new book covers are easy to make. The old cover is removed and new back and front sections are cut from similar weight card. These are covered with new cover material, and held in place with end papers.

Materials and equipment

Papers for covering books should be strong enough to resist creasing and cracking, and have a surface which does not mark easily. Wallpapers, specialist papers like marbled and other hand-made papers are ideal. These and artist's Ingres, Canson or cartridge (drawing) papers are suitable for making end papers.
Card such as artist's mounting board (mat board) is a suitable weight for most book covers.
Fabrics like closely woven cottons, chintz, silks or linen make attractive covers.
Leather and leather-look sticky backed plastics can be used to complement paper or fabric covers.
A ruler, set square (triangle) and pencil are needed for measuring and marking up the cover.
A craft knife or sharp scissors are used for cutting out the cover.
Adhesives such as stick adhesive, PVA (white glue) or clear craft glue are suitable for papers. For other materials use appropriate glue.

Covering a book

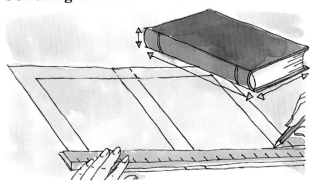

1 Measure the width and depth of the book cover, and the depth of the spine. Mark out the cover paper, allowing 2½in (6.5cm) round the drawn edge for overlaps. Cut out the cover. Extend the spine lines to the edge of the paper. (If using other material make a paper pattern.)

2 Lay the book open on the paper, line up spine with drawn outline to check fit and lightly trace around the book. Remove book. Cut from the top of the paper along the spine lines to the book outline. Fold in the resulting flaps and glue flat. To strengthen this area, cut a strip of cover material to the same size as the spine, and stick this over the flaps.

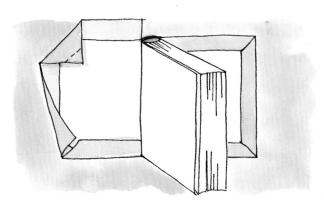

3 Lay the book on the cover, spines level and fit the corners over the book by making a diagonal fold as shown. Crease the fold line and trim some of the paper away. Fold in the flaps at the side, top and bottom and press flat. Stick the flaps to the inside of the cover or, if you want the cover to be removable, only stick them to the diagonal flap.

Making end pages

These hold the cover to the pages. The paper can be plain to blend with the pages, or in a colour or design to complement the book cover.

1 Measure the first page exactly, and draw this size on to the end paper. Extend these measurements so you have a shape to cover the inside of the book cover and the first page. Cut out, and repeat for the back page end papers.

2 Fold the sheet in half across its width, and spread glue evenly over one half. Line up the fold of the paper with the spine edge of the cover, and smooth the paper across the inside cover. Run a line of glue ½in (1cm) deep next to the fold line (shown by dotted line). Hold the cover vertically, and at the same time smooth the glued end paper on to the first page. Shut the book. Repeat for back, then place book under a heavy weight until glue dries.

Re-covering a book

Favourite books, whether genuinely old but tattered, or new but with uninspiring covers, can be transformed to look like traditionally bound books. Handmade marbled paper and leather are used to make the sophisticated book cover featured overleaf. Leather-look sticky backed plastic could be used as an economical substitute, or the idea could be copied in bright modern colours as a gift for a child.

You will need

◇ Artist's mounting board, or slightly heavier weight board
◇ Leather for spine and corners
◇ Marbled paper
◇ Ingres paper for end papers
◇ PVA (white glue) or craft adhesive
◇ Craft knife and metal cutting edge
◇ Scissors
◇ Set square (triangle), ruler and pencil
◇ Tape for bookmark
◇ Wide tape to reinforce book spine if necessary

1 Start by carefully removing the old cover. Trim away the end papers neatly, cutting along the fold line with a craft knife if necessary. The spine can be strengthened with glue and tape. Lay the book on top of your work bench so that the spine hangs just over the edge and weight it down. Spread a thin layer of glue along the spine, cut a length of tape to fit, and press this on to the glue. Leave to dry.

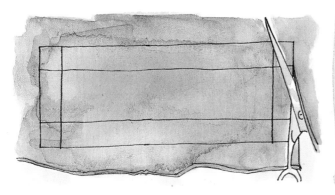

2 Take the measurements of the old front and back cover pieces and draw these on to card. Cut out, using a craft knife. Mark out the spine size on the wrong side of the leather. Allow an extra 1¼in (3cm) at each side of the spine, and ⅝in (1.5cm) overlap at both ends. Cut out:

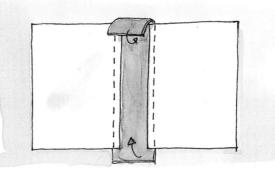

3 Put glue 1¼in (3cm) in from the spine, on each piece of card. Position the glued edges on to the leather spine, up to the drawn outline and ⅝in (1.5cm) down from the top. Spread glue on the spine overlaps at the top and bottom and press them over, level with the edges of the card.

4 Cut a strip of leather to line the spine, and glue in place. Cut four leather trapeziums to fit across the corners of the cover. Spread with glue, and stick in position. Make a small cut down the centre of each to the book corner, and fold to the wrong side.

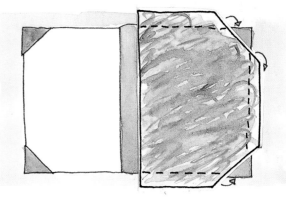

5 Cut rectangles from marbled paper, ¼in (6mm) narrower and 1¼in (3cm) longer than the size of the cardboard. Cut the paper off at an angle at the corners so that it just overlaps the leather trapeziums. Glue the paper overlaps to the wrong side. To make a bookmark, glue tape to the spine 1in (2.5cm) from top. Make end papers as before.

Making a portfolio

A rose-patterned cotton makes a pretty cover for a small portfolio. Use it to hold a collection of photos, keepsakes or writing paper.

You will need

◇ Cotton chintz or percale for cover
◇ Fabric or paper for lining
◇ ¾yd (60cm) 1in (2.5cm) wide tape or ribbon for the ties
◇ Fabric glue
◇ Cardboard
◇ Thick paper or thin card for flaps
◇ Craft knife, cutting edge, scissors

1 Cut two pieces of cardboard the size required for portfolio. Cut a slot for the ties at one short end of each piece of cardboard. To do this, mark the centre 1½in (4cm) in from a short edge. Using a craft knife, cut ½in (1cm) each side of the centre mark. Cut another line next to this to finish the slot.

2 Cut a piece of chintz large enough to cover both card pieces, with 2½in (6.5cm) for turnings and extra fabric for the spine fold. The depth of the spine fold is flexible but anything from 1½in (4cm) to 3in (7.5cm) will work. Place the card pieces in position on the wrong side of the fabric and draw round each of them lightly.

3 Spread glue on one side of each card piece, and press on to the wrong side of the fabric. Glue the turnings over on to the card, following the instructions for sticking the corners on page 69.

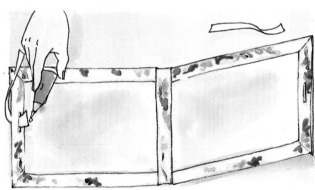

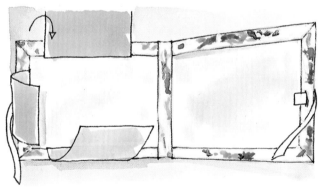

4 Cut a piece of fabric to cover the spine, wide enough to overlap the card slightly and the same length as the spine. Glue in place. Cut the tape into two pieces, and pierce the fabric along the tie slits. From the right side, push the tape ends through the slits, and glue the ends flat to the card.

5 To make the side flaps, cut two pieces of thick paper or thin card a little narrower than the width of the cover, and deep enough to curve round and support the portfolio contents. For the end flap, cut a piece as wide as the card still showing, and the same depth as the side flaps. Align the flap edges with the fabric, and run a line of glue ½in (1cm) wide along this line. Press the paper in place, and gently fold up the side flaps over the end flap.

6 Cut a piece of fabric or paper to make a lining, large enough to overlap the raw edges of the turnings. Spread glue on the wrong side of the lining, and smooth in place.

Paper chests

*Cardboard chests of drawers covered with
attractive papers have a multiplicity of uses which make them
ideal objects to give as presents. Use
them for holding stationery, sewing aids and jewellery, or
just for storing bits and pieces.*

Paper covered chests of drawers can be miniature copies of the real thing, complete with raised plinths and shaped tops, or they can be basic box shapes simply divided into sections to hold a series of boxes or 'drawers'. These can be of equal size or proportioned like a real chest, with smaller drawers at the top and a large bottom drawer.

The choice of paper used to cover the chest of drawers will influence the way it looks even more than its shape. A basic chest covered in a strong geometric pattern will have a completely different character from an identically-shaped one covered in a floral pastel coloured paper. The finished effect varies also if the drawers are covered in a colour that contrasts with the main chest. With these differences in mind you can create custom-made chests to suit any taste or age or to blend in with different colour schemes.

Materials and equipment

Strong card like Daler board or thick brown card should be used to make the basic chest shape. The card should be quite rigid so that it does not bow or distort when the drawers are opened.

Artist's mounting board is a good weight of card for the drawers, which should be made from slightly thinner card than the main chest.

Papers to cover the chest can be any type as long as they are strong enough to fold and stick over the card without tearing, rubbing or marking easily. The paper should be thick enough not to show what is underneath, so check this when choosing pale colours. Many giftwrap papers and wallpapers are quite suitable, as are handmade marbled papers, and specialist papers like fake leather and suede, or richly decorated Italian papers.

The insides of the drawers can be left uncovered, or lined with matching or contrast paper. A toning plain colour, or a smaller scale design to the main design can look most effective.

Handles for the drawers can be made from bobble buttons or beads stitched or wired through the drawer front, or from metal picture hangers available from craft suppliers. Small curtain rings held in place with split pin paper clips could substitute for these. Scaled down screw-in handles can be bought in some DIY shops or hobby specialists. Fabric tassels are another option; these look attractive used on single or large drawer chests. Choose a colour to tone with the paper.

Craft knife to cut the card should be a heavy duty type, which can also be used to cut the paper. Cut against a metal edge and use a protective surface under the card and paper when cutting out.

Adhesives such as a clear quick drying multi-purpose craft glue is used to stick the card. A low tack spray adhesive as sold for mounting photographs can be used to stick the paper to the card. This is quick and easy to use, but spray the paper in a spray booth made from an old box, to protect other surfaces from the sticky mist. Otherwise use wallpaper paste, but it is advisable to check the effect on the paper beforehand, as thin papers like giftwrap may become transparent when dampened.

Other materials needed are brown gummed paper tape for reinforcing the card edges, pencil, eraser, ruler, set square and scissors.

Stationery chest

The chest has two drawers and is a handy size for storing stationery. The top drawer is slim enough to hold notepaper, while the larger drawer can hold a generous supply of envelopes. The techniques used to make this chest can be successfully applied to any size chest, so you could adapt our design to make a chest with more drawers, or simply change the scale to make a larger or smaller model. The drawers themselves can be divided with slot-in card strips, to make storage compartments appropriate to the chest contents; to organise small items of stationery or jewellery or hobby requisites.

The chest of drawers measures 9in (23cm) wide by 7in (18cm) deep, and 3in (7.5cm) high. The drawers hold standard 8in (20.5cm) by 6in (15cm) size notepad and envelopes. Because card thicknesses vary, and the sizes of the drawers depend on the inside measurement of the basic shape, sizes for the drawers are not given in detail. Follow the step-by-step instructions for the technique, and you will be able to make drawers to accurately fit your own particular chest.

You will need
◇ Thick card for basic box
◇ Thinner card for drawers
◇ Paper to cover drawers and lining paper
◇ Clear craft adhesive
◇ Spray adhesive or wallpaper paste
◇ Brown gummed paper tape
◇ Heavy duty craft knife and cutting surface
◇ Scissors, pencil, eraser, ruler and set square
◇ Two handles of choice

Making the chest

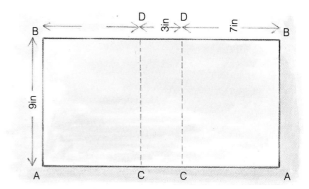

1 Draw out chest top, back and base on to card as shown. Gently score along lines C to D and fold card into shape along these lines.

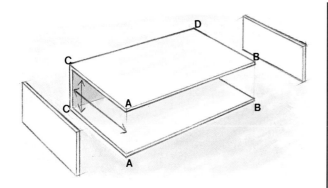

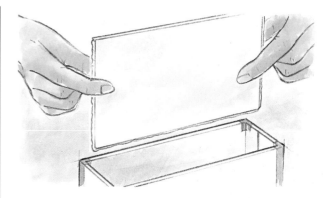

2 Take the inside measurement between point C and C and measure from the inside of the card from C to A. Draw these sizes out twice on to card, to make the chest sides. Cut out.

3 Run a line of glue along the long edges and one short edge of each side section, and fit them in place, making sure all sides are completely flat and level. Press to stick and leave to dry.

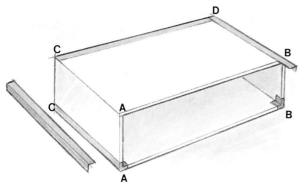

4 Reinforce the scored lines and the joined edges with strips of gummed paper tape. Cut lengths of tape to fit exactly the lines C to D. Fold the tape in half lengthways. Stick in position. Cut extra lengths of tape to cover the sides A to C and B to D, lining them up exactly with the back edge, and allowing a little to overlap the front open edge. Fold and stick in place as before, turning overlap to the wrong side.

5 Mark the position for the top drawer support. Draw a line two thirds up on the inside of the box. Repeat this step on the other side of the box. Now take the measurement of the space between these two lines across the box front, and the depth of the line from the inside back of the chest. Draw out a rectangle on a piece of card to this size and cut out.

6 Run a line of glue along the back and side edges of the card. Tip the box on its back and carefully slide the support into position along the drawn line. Leave till dry. Cut four strips of gummed tape exactly to the depth of the support. Fold in half lengthways, sticky side outwards and stick in place on top and under both sides of the drawer support.

Covering the chest

1 Measure round the top, sides and base of the chest, and draw this measurement on to the back of your chosen paper. Add an extra ½in (1.2cm) to the length as an overlap. Mark out the box depth 7in (18cm) and add ¾in (2cm) to each side of this for overlaps. Cut out.

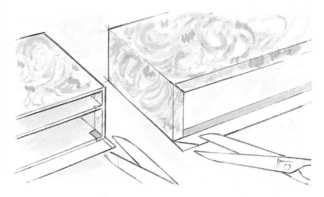

2 Either spray the back of the paper with adhesive, or brush over with wallpaper paste. Align one short edge with the base line of the chest, and carefully smooth the paper over the chest. Press overlap to base of chest. Carefully snip paper at each of the four front corners, and press paper to the inside. Snip paper each side of the drawer support and press to inside. Smooth remaining central section along support front, pressing excess to each side. Snip into the overlaps at the back, and trim as shown. Press flat.

3 Cover back of chest. Measure back, and draw shape onto the wrong side of paper. Cut out ⅛in (3mm) inside drawn line, so that paper covers overlaps neatly without reaching to back edges.

4 Cut a strip of paper 2½in (6.5cm) wide by inside width of box support. Glue and position along support edge, press flat.

Making the drawers

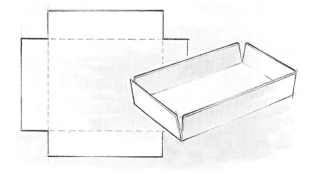

1 To make the drawers, take the inside measurements of the width and depth of the drawer space and mark these on to thin card to make the base. Draw out the rectangle, just inside the measurements, to allow for ease of fit. Measure the height of the drawer space, and add these measurements to the base. Cut out, score along fold lines and bend into shape. Try out fit of drawers in chest, and trim if fit is tight. Glue edges of drawers together, and reinforce with brown tape.

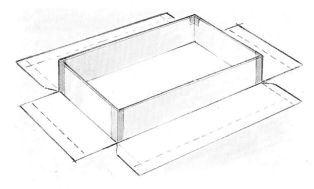

2 To cover drawers, lay the drawer on wrong side of a sheet of paper and draw a pencil line round base shape. Use ruler and set square to extend these lines to depth of drawer sides. Add a ¾in (2cm) overlap along top edge, and draw ½in (1cm) side overlaps as shown. Cut out.

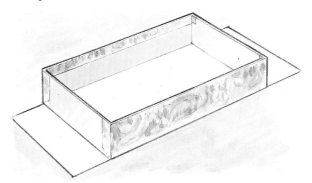

3 Glue wrong side of paper and place drawer centrally. Smooth front and back sections in place, pressing overlaps flat. Smooth side sections in place.

▷ *Two marbled paper designs have been used to cover this chest. The brass handles add a smart touch.*

TIP	SCENTED LINING PAPER

Make a scented chest of drawers as a special gift. Cover the chest or line the drawers with scented drawer lining paper. The drawers could hold a matching pot pourri, or notepaper.

Adding handles

Whatever style you choose, the handle will have to be fixed right through the drawer front. If using bobble buttons or beads, use a strong needle and thread to stitch through the card.

1 Mark the handle position centrally and pierce through the card with a bradawl, compass or other sharp point. Insert the handle fitting and attach as appropriate.

2 Neaten inside drawer by covering fixings with a strip of gummed paper tape. If drawer is to be unlined, neaten by covering inside front edge with a strip of the covering paper.

Lining drawers

Drawer linings add a neat and practical finishing touch to your chest of drawers.

1 Measure the depth of the drawer sides, and measure out four strips of paper to this depth. Add ½in (1cm) overlaps on short sides of two pieces, cut out and stick these in place. Position the linings with the tops just below the edge of the drawer, so the paper overlaps the base slightly.

2 Add the two other side linings, pressing the paper firmly into each corner. Cut a piece of paper to fit the base, and glue this into position.

Making paper

Making your own paper, whether it's made from recycled pulp or freshly gathered plants and fibres, is an exciting and rewarding pastime. Simple household equipment is all that is needed to produce unusual textured and scented papers which can be used in a variety of attractive ways.

Paper making is an ancient craft with its origins in China and Egypt. Natural fibres like cotton, hemp and flax were the traditional materials used to make paper long before wood pulp, which is used today for most paper making, was discovered as a readily available basic ingredient.

Although paper making has been mechanized for centuries, the basic stages are the same for making mass-produced and handmade papers. Paper is made from a pulp obtained by soaking vegetable matter or used paper until the fibres separate. A framed mesh which acts as a sieve is trawled across the pulp, the contents are drained, and the resulting residue dries to form a sheet of paper.

Handmade papers

Specially made papers have always been in demand for use as artist's watercolour papers, for bookbinding and for quality documents. A growing awareness of conservation needs has resulted in a fresh interest in recycled and handmade papers. The most familiar recycled papers are newspapers and paper bags. However, recycling does not necessarily mean reduced quality. By adding new and unusual materials it is possible to make very attractive quality papers.

Raw materials

The colour and the quality of any paper depends on the type of material used to make the pulp. As a beginner to paper making, it is easiest to start with a pulp made from readily available papers.

Tissues, computer print-out papers, used writing and typing papers, artist's papers, old drawings and watercolour paintings, book pages, blotting paper, and paper bags are some of the papers that can be used to make a basic pulp. Avoid magazine pages and papers with glossy or oily surfaces, as the chemicals in these make them unsuitable. Likewise, avoid newspapers, as the ink discolours the finished paper.

△ *One of the most popular ways to use handmade papers is to fold them for use as greetings cards*

Scented and coloured papers

The papers shown overleaf illustrate the range of effects you can achieve by adding different materials to the basic pulp. Fresh or dried flowers and leaves, vegetables, fabric threads, stamped out paper shapes and shreds of fabric all add great variety.

Fragrant herbs and leaves, pot pourri, lavender or rose petals can be added to make extra special papers, although the scent will fade as the paper dries. The pulp can be coloured by adding natural vegetable dyes made by boiling red cabbage or onion skins, or with tea or coffee. Fabric dyes suitable for cotton can also be used to give bright colours. Two-tone and marbled effects can be achieved by mixing different coloured pulps together.

Key

1 Covered frame	**6** Leaves and petals
2 Plain frame	**7** Liquidizer (blender)
3 Lavender	**8** Chopping board
4 Selection of paper	**9** Palette knife
5 Bucket	**10** Kitchen cloth
	11 Washing up bowl

Using handmade papers

A collection of attractive and unique papers can be used in many different ways. Apart from use as drawing or writing papers, they can be used as mounts for pictures, stitched together to make books, and if the texture is fine enough to bend easily, to cover books or pads. Handmade papers can also be used with other crafts. Papier mâché, or découpage and collage could all be worked using these papers.

Materials and equipment

Besides the scrap paper for the pulp and a collection of materials for decorating the paper, such as patterned or coloured papers, threads, flowers, or leaves, there are few special pieces of equipment required, apart from the frames.

Two equal sized frames are used to trawl and press the paper. These can be made up from 1in x 1½in (25mm x 38mm) timber, or picture frames can be used instead. The corners must be secured firmly with screws or nails to withstand immersion in water. A piece of mesh, such as net curtaining, is stapled or pinned to one of the frames. The finer the mesh, the smoother the paper will be. A coarse mesh will allow more of the pulp material to remain on the surface.

An electric liquidizer (blender) is used for refining the pulp.

A plastic bucket is used to soak the selection of papers used to make the pulp.

A plastic bowl a little larger than the frames is used to hold the prepared pulp.

You will also need a palette knife to help lift the damp paper from the frame; absorbent kitchen cloths to blot the newly made paper, and flat boards like pastry or chopping boards to weight the paper to flatten it. Have plenty of spare newspapers or plastic sheeting to protect the floor and work surfaces.

Preparing the frames

One of the frames used for paper making is left empty. This provides an edge to shape the paper. The other frame, covered with mesh, is held under the empty one, and this picks up the pulp and holds it flat to form the sheet of paper.

1 Cut a piece of mesh fabric, large enough to reach over the frame to the other side. Lay the frame over this, lining up the straight grain of the fabric with the edge of the frame.

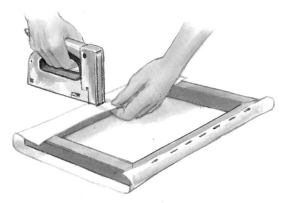

2 Starting at the centre and working outwards, staple the fabric to the frame. At each corner fold the fabric over to fit, and staple securely so that the mesh is taut and even. Trim excess fabric.

Making the pulp

It is a good idea to make small amounts of pulp to start with, so that you can experiment with different ingredients to create different effects. Changes in thickness or colour and texture can then be made without wasting time or materials. Keep a note of the ingredients used so you can re-create the effect if you are happy with the results. Any extra pulp can be stored for about one week in a refrigerator, after which it will start to rot.

1 Rip up a selection of papers into small pieces or strips. You must tear rather than cut, so that the water can penetrate the paper. Soak them overnight in a bucket of clean cold water. This soaking swells and loosens the fibres in the paper.

2 Pour off any soaking water which has not been absorbed, and add the pulp a tablespoon at a time, to the liquidizer. Add water, so that the goblet is three quarters full. Run the liquidizer for about quarter of a minute, then check that the pulp is evenly mashed. Rearrange the pulp as necessary, and switch on for another five seconds or so until the pulp is even. Tip the pulp into the plastic bowl.

3 Flowers, leaves and other materials can be added to the last batch of pulp half way through the liquidizing proces. Experiment with these additions, as some materials can be stirred in without liquidizing, or pressed on to the still wet paper if desired. Do not mix fine materials like flower petals and leaves in the liquidizer for too long, if you wish them to retain their shape. Silk threads should be cut as they are too tough for most liquidizers.

Making a sheet of paper

1 Gently stir the pulp, and wait for the water movement to cease. Do not allow the pulp to settle, as this will make it difficult to gather up. Hold the frames together at the sides, with the mesh covered frame, mesh upwards, underneath the empty frame. Holding the frames firmly, and at the far side of the bowl, slide them under the water.

2 Keeping the frames steady and quite flat, lift them from the water. A layer of pulp should completely cover the mesh. Hold the frames so that some of the water can drain away.

> **◆ TIP   IRONING PAPER**
>
> Paper sheets can be ironed after flattening to obtain a smooth finish. Place the paper between two sheets of clean paper or cotton fabric, and press with a medium heat. If this is done when the paper is still slightly damp, the texture of the pressing paper or cloth will imprint itself on the surface.

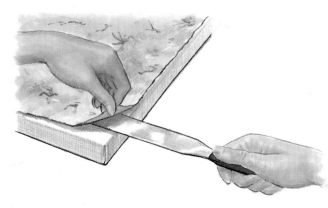

3 Remove the empty frame. At this stage extra details like paper cut-outs can be pressed in to the wet surface. Use a palette knife to help loosen the paper on the frame.

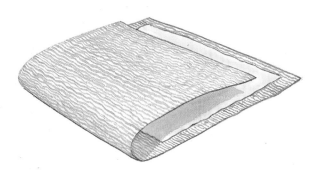

4 Tip the paper on to one half of a flattened kitchen cloth and turn up the other end to cover the paper. Continue adding freshly made sheets of paper and kitchen cloths in this way, then weight the pile between two boards to squeeze out the excess water. Carefully separate the paper leaves when they are dry.

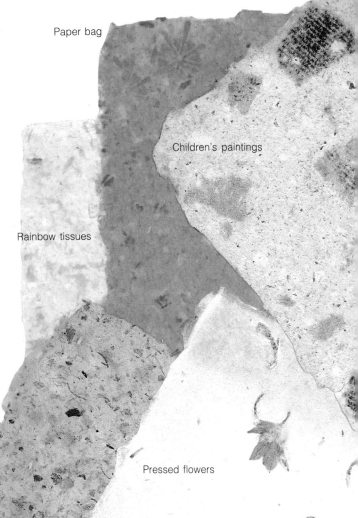

Paper bag

Children's paintings

Rainbow tissues

Pot pourri

Hole-punched paper and tissues

Silk threads

Pressed flowers

Embossed paper

*Embossing is engraving or moulding in relief.
A wide range of decorative effects — from all-over designs to
small motifs — can be created by pressing
selected objects into damp paper. The technique is ideal for
designing personalized gift cards and stationery.*

Embossing adds another dimension to a flat piece of paper. The technique is worked on wet paper — either on the pulp as the paper is made, or on a paper sheet dampened sufficiently for the fibres to wrap round and cling to a selected object.

Embossed images can be created in a number of ways using different techniques; a basic method is to press an object into the paper, then remove it. For a well-defined embossed motif, the embossing tool must be left in position until the paper is completely dry. Many of the embossing tools mentioned here, like metal objects, fibres and fabrics, are suitable for this simple embossing method. An alternative method of embossing is to trap the embossing object permanently between two thin layers of paper pulp.

For details on paper-making techniques, see pages 77-80.

Materials and equipment

In addition to papermaking materials mentioned on pages 77-80, you will need:

Laundry starch

Add a solution of laundry starch to the basic pulp to produce a smooth paper that is easy to write on.

Ready-made papers

Ready-made papers and thin card can be used to give embossed designs on other paper and as the background paper to receive the embossed design. Both the papers and the card must be dampened before they can be embossed.

Embossing tools

Cotton lace or **net** with bold crunchy textures — both create attractive embossed effects. These materials can be used to create all-over patterns, or lace motifs can be chosen for small designs.
Metal objects Use keys, chains, rings and wire mesh to create strong outlines. They can also be used to emboss all-over or selected images.
Printing blocks are traditionally used to mark the patterns on cloth and can also emboss sharply defined images on paper.
Coloured card and **thick paper** can be used for a dual purpose — to give an imprint (shiny card will leave a glossy imprint) and to give a subtle tint. To check how the card or paper will shed its colour, soak a test sample in cold water for an hour.
Other objects Fabric scraps, haberdashery cords, braids, plant seeds and fibres will all create interesting impressions in the paper.

Low-relief embossing

Using printing blocks

Make a sheet of thick paper (or required number) and press to remove excess moisture. Open the couching cloth and fold it to create a double layer under the paper. Lay cloth and paper on to a thick layer of folded newspapers.

Position the printing block on the damp paper surface and apply pressure. Use clothes pegs on two corners and hang paper up to dry.

▷ *Printing blocks pressed on to damp paper achieve a really professional result.*

To emboss paper

1 Scoop wet pulp on to frame and allow to drain. When nearly dry, transfer sheet to drying cloth and press under weights. While still damp, unwrap and press embossing tool in position. Cover with cloth.

2 Press the cloth under heavy weights until it is almost dry. Dry each embossed sheet separately, to avoid the danger of different images pressing down on top of one another.

3 Finish off drying by pressing the paper, (with embossing tool and drying cloth still in place), with a hot iron. Press until dry.

Using coloured card

Cut card into strips, or cut and punch into a design motif or band. Lay in position on damp paper, wrap with couching cloth and press to dry. For best results leave the card in place until paper is dry.

Drying can be speeded up by hanging paper in its cloth to dry, or by pressing it with an iron.

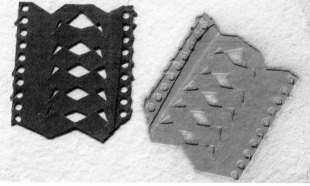

Embossing with lace
Air drying method

Stretch lace tightly across paper-making frame or circular embroidery hoop, taking care not to distort lace pattern. Hold the deckle (empty top frame) or the outer ring of the hoop between finger and thumb of each hand and scoop through the prepared paper pulp. Leave the whole apparatus to drain on newspapers. When drained, tilt the frame slightly and finish drying in an airy place. Do not attempt to remove paper until completely dry.

When dry, gently ease a pointed palette knife under the paper and separate it from the lace. The paper will have taken an impression from the lace texture.

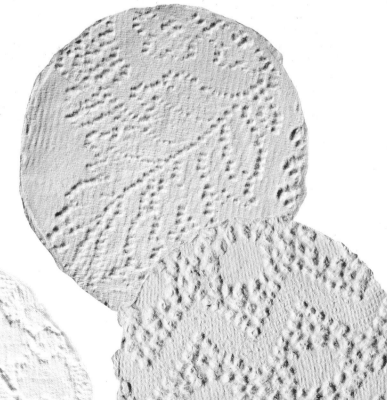

Lace sandwich design

With this technique the lace or broderie anglaise is trapped between two thin layers of paper.

To work, make a sheet of paper and lay the lace strip or motif over the damp pulp. Make another paper sheet from the same, or contrasting pulp. Drain both, then carefully remove from their frames. Place lace-covered sheet on kitchen cloth and place plain paper sheet on top. Cover with cloth and press layers firmly with weights until dry. The pattern will be visible on both sides of the paper. Samples are shown, right.

▽ *This exquisitely embossed Victorian Valentine card bears the message, 'I love you'.*

Using strip lace

Stretch plain mesh across the frame, incorporating a strip of broderie anglaise or heavy lace as desired, to create a raised border design.

Emboss lace motifs by first securing them to the mesh with small stitches. Continue the process as for making paper, and dry on a frame as for other lace.

▽ *Paper with strip lace.*

Folders

*Transform folders and envelopes into
more than just functional containers by making them from
specially selected cards and papers. Add
attractive and practical details using simple stationery
fastenings and dressmaking tools and trims.*

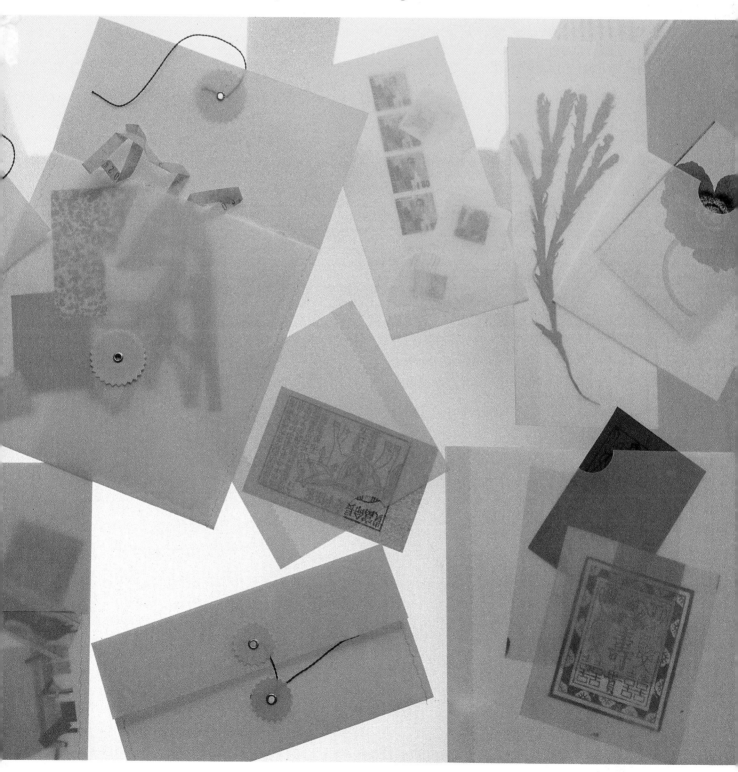

Keep small, easy-to-lose items like tickets, press cuttings, bills, snapshots and special momentos safe and easy to find in specially made folders, pockets, envelopes and mini portfolios. Choose transparent papers for contents you need to identify quickly and decorative handmade papers for special gift-wrapped style envelopes.

One of the advantages of making your own envelopes is size — they can be made to exactly the required proportions. The tiniest special scrap of paper can be secured in as plain or decorative a folder as you wish; and larger collections can also be accommodated.

Materials and equipment

Papers Tracing papers are available in different weights. For envelope making, choose between 90g and 180g weights as these are strong and handle well. Thin card and mottled vellum papers, Oriental papers, textured art papers and handmade papers, with a rich grainy surface, make eye-catching folders. You can use any paper which creases easily to a fold and is strong enough for its purpose. Attractive light-weight papers can be folded and, if necessary, used double thickness for added strength.

Fasteners Stationery fasteners like brass split pins and cord 'treasury' tags provide an alternative to glued edges or sticky tape, and can become a decorative feature in their own right. Dressmaking eyelets can be used to join edges and anchor strengthening discs of card or paper for closure ties on envelopes.

Fixing and cutting tools Pinking shears make attractive serrated cut edges — useful for cutting discs or trimming turnings. Eyelets are available in a variety of sizes and colours. The special tool for fixing these is often included in the eyelet pack, while some eyelets are attached with a hammer. A hole punch or a belt hole punch gives a professional look to holes made for fastenings. A wad punch has an advantage over other types of punch as it can be positioned anywhere on the paper and is sold with different fittings, which punch holes in a variety of sizes.

Adhesives Spray adhesive is ideal for adding paper linings and flaps to card portfolios, and for securing side flaps on transparent papers. PVA and any clear-drying craft glue can be used for general glueing.

Ties Choose materials to complement the colour and texture of the paper. Thin cords and string, twine, raffia, glittery giftwrap string, embroidery threads and narrow ribbon all make attractive ties. Use sticky paper reinforcement rings as decorative trims to surround and strengthen the punched holes used for ties. Lace narrow hat elastic through punched holes and eyelets to join folder sides and make integral ties. Edges can also be stitched together. Use coloured thread or 'invisible' nylon sewing thread and a straight or zigzag machine stitch; or vary the effect with a decorative embroidery stitch.

You will also need sharp scissors, a craft knife, set square, compass, pencil, eraser and ruler.

Simple pocket envelopes

Make pocket envelopes from see-through paper (like the ones in our pictures) and in any shape or size. Use the pattern (right) as a guide, or make your own template. To do this: draw a strip as wide as the desired envelope by twice the finished length; mark the foldline. Add tabs to the depth of each folded side and (optional) a top flap. Cut a curve in the centre of the straight top edge (or both if no flap is included) for easy access to the folder's contents.

Cut out, using scissors, then trim the flap edges with pinking shears for a decorative edge. Gently crease the fold lines and bend the flaps to the back. Secure the flaps to the back envelope with adhesive (mask other areas if using spray adhesive). Alternatively, to secure flaps, punch holes through all layers and attach split-pin fasteners or corded tags.

▽ *Special cards and delicate papers are best kept in transparent paper wallets for easy identification.*

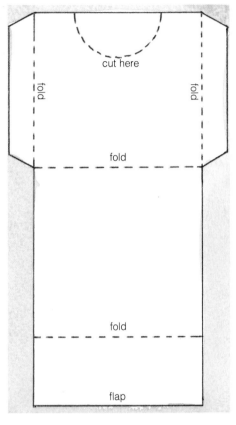

Envelopes

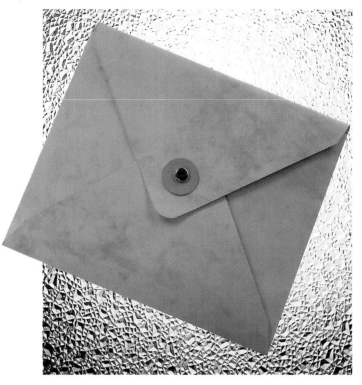

These can be made by simply folding a sheet of paper into three. The sides can be sewn together, punched and laced, or held together with paper fasteners, decorative ribbon, fine elastic or string.

Make envelopes with large un-glued side flaps and generously sized overlaps to hold bulkier contents. Enlarge or reduce the pattern as necessary to make an envelope of the required size. Cut out the shape and crease along fold lines. Mark position on each large end flap for fastening disc.

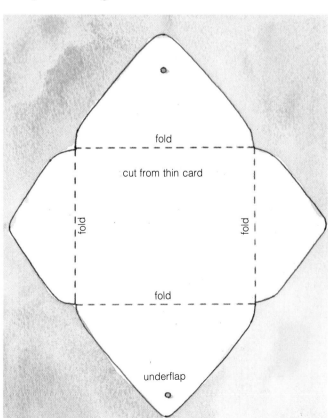

Portfolios

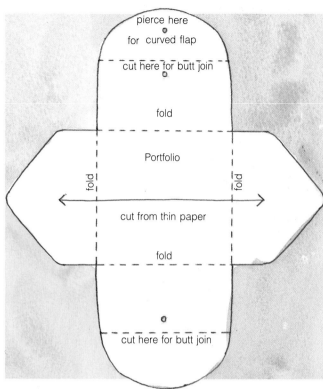

Copy the basic pattern given (above) to make a portfolio with flaps that butt together at the centre or, alternatively, flaps with a curved edge that overlap. The portfolio can be lined with contrasting paper or cut from a single sheet of decorative paper.

Add discs and eyelets for fastening ties, or use eyelets on their own to make a portfolio with butt-joined flaps. Ties made from lengths of cord, string or ribbon can be attached to the disc and wound round the portfolio to give a more decorative look.

TIP	LINING A PORTFOLIO

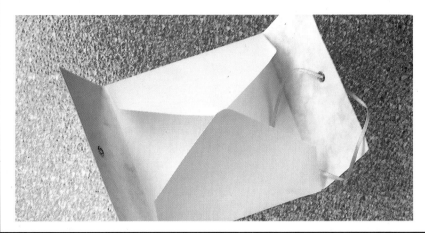

If the card used for the portfolio is heavy, make the inner flaps from a lighter paper or card to prevent the portfolio from being too bulky.

This is easily done in the following way: cut the portfolio in two sections; cut the base and two top flaps in one strip from the heavier card; then cut the inner flaps and base in one strip from the lighter card. Glue the lighter card to the inside, carefully aligning the base sections.

Fastening discs

Discs of paper can be used as novelty fasteners on any of the envelope styles shown here. The discs can be held in place with eyelets, metal fasteners or ties. Make the discs from matching or contrasting paper; or, if the discs are to be fastened with ties, make sure you make them from a card that is firm enough to hold the ties securely without becoming bent.

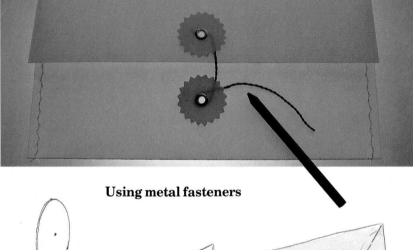

Making the discs

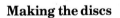

Using metal fasteners

To make a disc, cut a square or circle from paper or card and mark the centre. Make a decorative edge on the disc by carefully cutting round the outline with pinking shears. Position the blades so that they align with the previously made zigzag edge at each cut, to produce an evenly serrated outline.

Spread a little adhesive on one side of a paper disc and press it in position. Use a punch to make a hole through all the centres. Stick another paper disc on the under flap to match and punch hole in the same way. Insert the fastener through both holes and secure by opening it flat underneath.

Using eyelets

Pierce a small hole through the centre of the disc, making sure the hole is slightly smaller than the diameter of the eyelet. Spread a small amount of adhesive around the centre hole to temporarily secure a paper disc on the envelope flap. Place the eyelet in the eyelet tool and fit in hole. Apply pressure as directed to squeeze eyelet into place so it firmly grips the back of the flap.

Marbling

*Marbling is a highly decorative technique used
to embellish paper, fabric and three-dimensional objects. The
simplest technique involves decorating paper and
the finished designs can be used as wrapping paper or to transform
boxes and other small items.*

The art of marbling is an ancient one which probably originated in Japan. The patterns are made by floating colours on a liquid and then transferring them to paper, fabric or small objects. It should not be confused with the more sophisticated paint effect of the same name, which uses paint and brushes to simulate marble.

The technique is best suited to paper, although it is possible to marble small objects, such as candles or blown eggs. To marble fabric a different, more advanced method must be used.

Each marbled pattern is unique and cannot be duplicated. Once the floating colours have been lifted from the surface, the design cannot be repeated and new colours are used for the next piece of marbling.

Using oil and water

This is the simplest way to marble and is ideal for creating lively patterns in which accidental colour combinations and patterns contribute effectively to the end result.

The technique involves floating oil paint on water (that is preferably at room temperature). As oil and water don't mix, the colours remain on the surface of the water and are then simply lifted off.

The paint is normaly dropped on to the surface using a pipette or artist's brush. However, you can create a bolder effect by pouring the paint on to the water.

When dropped into the water the paint should rise to the surface and spread out to form a disc. Although you can vary the consistency of the paint, ideally it should be the thickness of single cream. If it is too thick it will simply sink.

Once on the surface, the paint can be teased into a variety of random pattern effects by moving it around with a thin stick or blowing gently across the surface with a drinking straw. A wide-toothed marbling comb drawn over the surface gives a distinctive swirling effect.

Using size

For more detailed and defined marble patterns, the paint can be floated on to size (a very thin wallpaper paste) instead of water. Although the principle is the same, the thicker medium gives you more control over the finished effect as it prevents the paint from moving around so freely. Size should be used at room temperatures.

Materials and equipment
Paint

Oil-based paints, such as artist's oil paints are ideal. They are available from most art shops and as they have to be thinned with a little white spirit before use, a little goes a long way.

Size

You can buy wallpaper or artist's size (methylcellulose sizing) from specialist outlets. Or make your own gelatine size (see right).

Container

You can use any watertight container as long as it is large enough to take your chosen paper. Try using a large baking tin, developing tray or cat litter tray.

Paper

Marbling works well on all types of paper except those that are very thin or exceptionally thick. Typing paper is ideal and a manageable size. Brown parcel paper, cartridge papers (drawing papers), or one of the many tinted papers, available from artist's suppliers and good stationers, can also be used.

Tools

The only tools you will need are a palette or small jars for mixing paint, old paint brushes, and a thin stick, knitting needle or wide-toothed comb for pattern making (turn over the page for instruction on making a marbling comb).

TIP   GELATINE SIZE

To make a gelatine size, dissolve a tablespoonful of gelatine powder in 1pt (600ml) of hot water. Thin with another 1pt (600ml) of cold water and allow to cool. The mixture should resemble a thin liquid, rather than jelly.

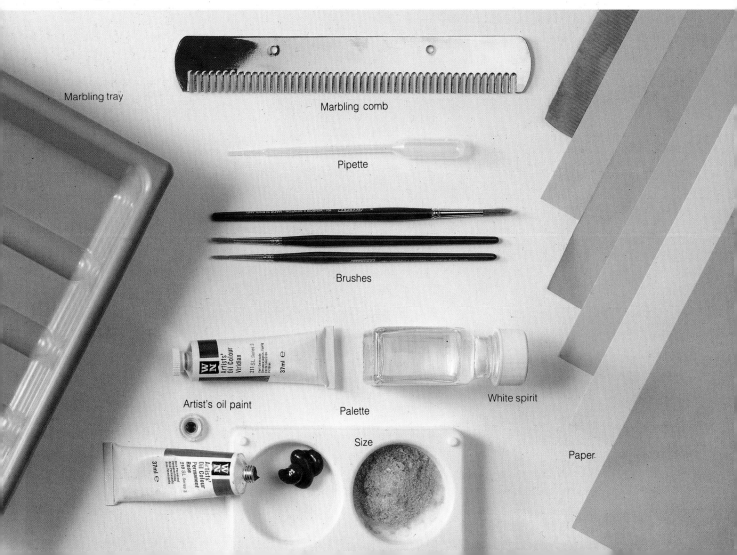

Marbling tray

Marbling comb

Pipette

Brushes

Artist's oil paint

Palette

White spirit

Size

Paper

Marbling paper

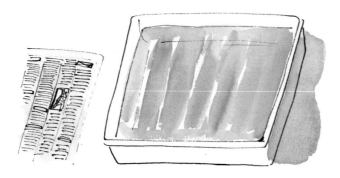

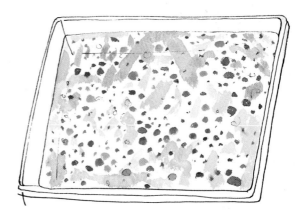

1 Half fill a container with water (or size mixture) and place several sheets of newspaper close to it, ready to receive the wet marbled sheet. Squeeze a little artist's oil colour into a palette or small jar and mix with white spirit. The colour should be the approximate consistency of single cream.

2 Drop spots of colour on to the water. The colour will spread out to form discs on the surface; the thinner the colour, the further it will spread. If the colour sinks to the bottom, it is too thick. Repeat with subsequent colours taking care not to overdo it; two or three colours are sufficient.

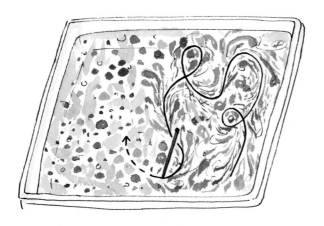

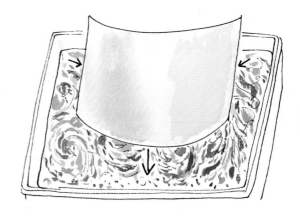

3 With a stick or knitting needle, blend and manipulate the colours. Alternatively, pull a wide-toothed comb across the surface to break up the colour into a distinctive feathered pattern.

4 When you have a pattern which pleases you, lower a sheet of paper on to the surface. To avoid air bubbles (which leave blank areas on the paper), hold the paper at either end and allow the curved centre of the sheet to touch the water first.

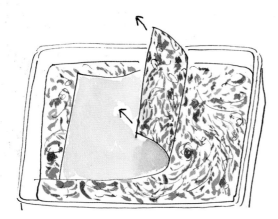

5 Carefully lift out the paper and place on newspaper. Some paint will remain on the water; you can often take a second or third print from this. Just tease the colours a little to blend them. Alternatively, remove the residue of colour by drawing a strip of newspaper across the surface before starting again.

6 The marbled paper will be dry enough to move after about half an hour. However, do not handle it too much as oil colour takes a long time to dry thoroughly (leave for at least a day). To flatten the finished work, weight it by covering it with plain paper and placing it between the pages of a large book.

Making a marbling comb

You can make a marbling comb
from thin card, pins or needles and
glue. Make several combs with
different tooth spacing.

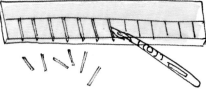
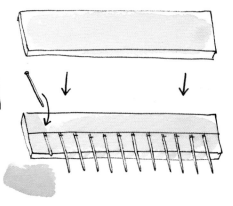

1 Cut two 2in (5cm) wide strips
of card to a length slightly
shorter than your marbling tray.
Draw a line, lengthways, down the
centre of one of the strips. On one
half, measure and mark out the
position of the teeth.

2 With a sharp scalpel, cut
shallow grooves from the
centre line to the edge of the card
— do not cut completely through
the card.

3 Press the needles into the slits
so that the sharp ends
protrude by at least 1in (2.5cm).
Firmly glue the second strip of card
on top of the first, enclosing the
needles. Finally, seal with a coat of
varnish or PVA adhesive.

Decorative desk set

For this beautiful desk set, you can
re-cover items that you already
have or you can make your own
from cardboard. Blue, green and
red were used for the marbling
shown here.

To make your own desk set,
choose stiff card and use a metal
ruler and, a sharp craft knife for
cutting. Corners and joins should
be stuck with a suitable strong
adhesive.

You will need
◇ Marbled paper
◇ Adhesive (not water-based)
◇ Craft knife
◇ Metal ruler
◇ Desk set

To make the desk set
Marble the paper according to the
instructions on the previous page
and leave until thoroughly dry. Cut
the marbled paper to cover the
pencil holder, letter case and
blotter, allowing enough margin all
around for seams and corner folds.
Stick the marbled paper firmly in
position with adhesive.

Paper weaving

*Strips of paper can be woven just
like yarn or cloth to create a patterned fabric which can
be used for a variety of decorative projects.
Tablecovers, hangings, bags and folders are just some of
the many design options available.*

All kinds of papers can be woven, from papers bought specially for their colours and designs to pages torn from magazines and newspapers. Often the most unlikely choices can add a surprise element; accidents which give a completely unplanned but pleasing texture or colour contrast to a design.

Experiment by weaving a selection of paper strips in different widths and colours, and discover new plaids and checks you wish were available in cloth.

Different papers

Almost any type of paper can be cut into strips and woven, including card, thin newsprint or tissue paper. Try incorporating art papers, posters, book and magazine pages, stationery, comics, newspapers and sheets of giftwrap.

Papers of different weights can be used together, providing the warp (the strips running down the weave) is strong enough to support the weft (strips running across the weave). Thinner papers can also be supported by placing them over stronger strips, before weaving the two strips together as one.

If the finished design is to have a practical rather than purely decorative use, choose durable paper. Avoid papers which mark easily.

Materials and equipment

Papers: choose a wide selection so you can try out ideas.

Ruler and **pencil** are used to mark out the strips on to paper.

Scissors or a **craft knife** and **metal edge** to cut against are needed for preparing the strips.

Adhesive such as stick adhesive is ideal for securing woven ends.

Work space is important. A large table, or even the floor, can be used as a base for arranging the strips. Small projects can be worked on any flat surface.

Paper clips or **heavy books** are useful for holding ends of strips in place as you work.

Weaving techniques

An even basketweave is the simplest weaving technique to use for paper. Warp strips are laid side by side, and weft strips are then slotted in and out and over and under the warp strips.

1 Cut a number of paper strips to form the warp. Strips can be any manageable size, from ⅜in (1cm) wide to 2in (5cm). Lay them side by side with ends level to make the warp. Cut weft strips the same width as the warp strips, but slightly longer than the total width of the warp strips.

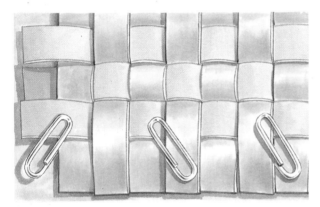

2 Weave a weft strip through the warp. Start by passing it over the first warp strip. Start the second weft strip by passing it under the first warp strip. Continue weaving in this way, gently pushing the weft strips together. If the warp strips slip, anchor them to the first weft line with paper clips or weigh them down with a heavy book.

3 If a strip is too short, lengthen it by joining it to another strip so that the join falls on the wrong side of the weave. Simply overlap the ends of the two strips and secure the join with adhesive. Slide the join out of sight.

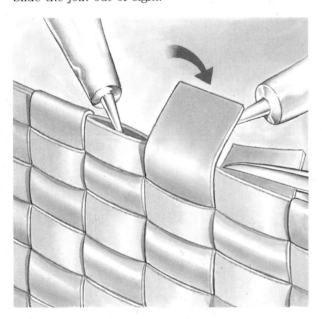

4 When the weaving is complete, secure the ends by folding them crisply to the wrong side along the edge of the last strip. Trim, leaving a turning at least the width of one strip. Spread adhesive on the back of the turning and press to the wrong side.

Woven paper cloth

The cloth in our picture is made with strips cut from sheets of patterned giftwrap paper. The design uses seven different patterned papers and five different coloured plain wrapping papers. The main body of the cloth is woven from equal size strips of the patterned papers, and the contrast border is worked in narrow strips of the plain paper. The finished cloth measures 63in (160cm).

You will need
◇ Two 20in (50cm) x 28in (70cm) sheets of wrapping paper in each of seven different designs
◇ One 20in (50cm) x 28in (70cm) sheet of plain wrapping paper in each of five different colours
◇ Adhesive stick

1 Cut patterned papers into strips measuring 2in (5cm) by 28in (70cm) strips, and plain papers into strips measuring 1in (2.5cm) by 28in (70cm). Cut four strips of each design in half, then join pieces with 1in (2.5cm) overlaps to make 68in (170cm) long strips (this takes two and a half strips).

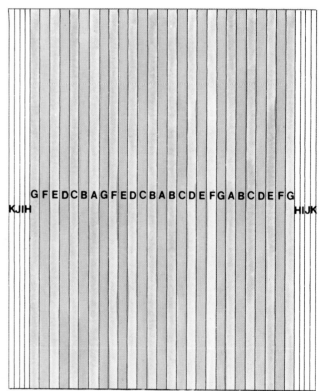

GFEDCBAGFEDCBABCDEFGABCDEFG
KJIH HIJK

ABCDEFG = 2in (5cm) wide strips of patterned paper
HIJK = 1in (2.5cm) wide strips of plain coloured paper

2 Line up the warp strips on the floor in the sequence shown. Letters A to G represent the wide strips of patterned paper, letters H to K the plain narrow stripes. The weft sequence is the same.

3 Weave the patterned weft strips across the warp, using books or paper clips to prevent the warp strips from moving or gaping.

4 Weave the plain border strips and, as you weave, secure the ends with glue, sticking them over or under the last warp strip.

5 Trim the top strip ends to 2in (5cm) and fold them over to the wrong side. Secure with glue.

6 Trim away the remaining ends, cutting the strips level with the edges of the border strips.

Making woven containers

Flat areas of weaving can easily be folded over and joined up to make unusual lightweight containers such as bags and folders. This is done by weaving in and gluing the protruding weft ends after an area of weaving is complete.

1 Neaten the warp ends by trimming and gluing them to the wrong side of the weave as described in step 4 Weaving techniques. Then fold the weaving in half along the edge of a weft strip.

2 Along the open sides, secure all the strips woven under a warp strip by gluing them to the wrong side of the weaving. Trim ends close to the edge.

3 Trim the remaining strips to the same width as the warp strips. Then fold over the edge and glue to the back of the trimmed strips.

Stationery tote set

These simple tote bags are woven from a mixture of ruled notepaper, an old map and brown wrapping paper decorated with postage stamps. With the addition of some colour-coordinated stationery they make an amusing and original gift.

When finished, the large tote bag measures about 11in (28cm) by 13in (33cm) and the small tote bag 4¼in (11cm) by 5½in (14.5cm).

You will need
◇ Ruled notepaper in four pastel shades
◇ Brown wrapping paper
◇ World map
◇ Assorted stamps
◇ Adhesive stick
◇ Paper gum
◇ Selection of pencils

Large tote bag

1 Glue stamps at random over the brown paper, using paper gum. Leave to dry completely.

2 Cut all the papers into 1in (2.5cm) strips, and join them up to make 31½in (80cm) lengths.

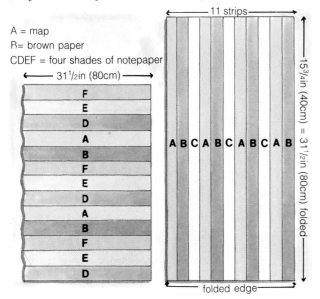

A = map
B= brown paper
CDEF = four shades of notepaper

31½in (80cm)

11 strips

ABCABCABCAB

15¾in (40cm) = 31½in (80cm) folded

folded edge

3 Take eleven prepared strips and fold them in half. Put them on a large work surface and arrange the strips in the sequence shown. Make sure that the folded edges are level.

4 Carefully weave the top layer with thirteen weft strips in the order shown in step 3, starting from the fold line and working upwards. Leave 2in (5cm) ends at the left side.

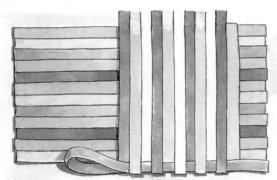

5 Carefully turn the work over, making sure that none of the woven strips slip out of position. Then continue weaving in the rest of the weft strips to the remaining warp strips.

6 Secure the open sides of the tote bag by gluing, trimming and folding the weft ends neatly in place. To do this, follow the instructions in steps 1 and 2 Making woven containers.

7 Neaten the top edge of the bag as for the woven paper cloth, steps 5 and 6, trimming the folded ends to a width of 1in (2.5cm).

8 Make handles from two 2in (5cm) by 11¾in (30cm) strips of brown paper. Fold in ¾in (2cm) along one side, then fold in ½in (1cm) on other side and glue down. Glue inside the bag top, and strengthen by covering the base of the handles with 2in (5cm) by 6in (15cm) strips of brown paper.

Small tote bag

This is made in the same way as the large bag, but with scaled down proportions: the strips are ½in (1.2cm) wide by 13¾in (35cm) long.

Leave weft ends protruding for 1in (2.5cm) at open side of bag, and trim to warp width as tote sides are joined. The handles are made from strips measuring 1in (2.5cm) by 4¾in (12cm) brown paper, folded in ½in (1cm) along one side, and ¼in (6mm) on the other. Omit the strengthening strip.

Covered pencils

Simply cut a length of paper to fit round the pencil and trim to fit allowing for a small overlap. Glue the back of the paper and smooth round the pencil. Press firmly until the glue dries.

Weaving variations

A wide range of different pattern effects can be achieved by alternating wide and narrow paper strips. Alternatively, try weaving together a mixture of contrasting plain papers and patterned papers.

Newspaper strips woven with a chequered paper make an interesting monotone design.

Create a richly textured weave by incorporating strips of paper cut from the pages of glossy magazines. For a subtle effect, choose pages where the colours are closely matched: for a bolder effect, cut strips from pages with greater colour contrasts.

To work a bold grid pattern, weave narrow weft strips across a warp made from both wide and narrow strips of paper.

Paper collage

*Collage is created by arranging and sticking
scraps of cut and torn, coloured or printed papers to produce an
abstract or figurative design. The technique can be
used in many unusual and diverse ways, to make large scale
murals or smaller eye-catching pictures.*

Like painting or drawing, collage is a wonderful way to express yourself visually. It is a very free medium, which, unlike painting and drawing, is an advantage for people who are not confident about their artistic abilities. The readily available supply of printed, coloured images to choose from provides the opportunity to handle colour and shape with more confidence. With a few guidelines you can cut out and experiment with patterns and

colours, rearranging them until you build up a pleasing composition.

Planning a collage

Start off with a basic idea of the effect you want to create. Your idea could come from a picture you have seen, a view, a photograph, or something imaginary. When planning a collage make sure that you have a good collection of papers to work with. Use these as you would a paint palette, and as your design

progresses, allow the colours and shapes of the papers in the collage to inspire you with fresh ideas.

Small areas of print and pattern can be used selectively to add a touch of realism to a composition. For instance, a newspaper can be represented with columns cut from newsprint, and clothing can be

▽ *All the bustle and atmosphere
of a busy launderette is captured in
this amusing and colourful collage.*

98

emphasized with woven or furry printed textures. Entire objects or figures can be cut from photographs and placed in the collage as well.

Plan the shape and balance of the collage as you work: fill in background and larger areas first, adding intricate shapes and details last. A tracing or rough sketch with colour notes for the finished collage will help with each stage.

Materials and equipment

Cards and papers The backing for the collage should be thick white card, such as artists' mounting board. Papers used for the collage should all be of a similar thickness, to help balance on the design. Plain papers and wrapping papers are useful for working the backgrounds and colour blending. Photographs taken from magazines, colour supplements, catalogues and posters offer a great variety of patterns and textures, but these should be broken down into small pieces, so that their original identity does not dominate the collage.

Adhesives Stick adhesive and clear petroleum gum are easy to spread and good for sticking papers. A hot wax roller, available from artwork or graphic suppliers is ideal for sticking paper shapes, as it allows you to reposition shapes while working the design; both the collages featured here were worked using this tool. If you intend to develop your collage skills, a hot wax roller is a good investment.

Scissors and blades in a variety of sizes are needed. Use manicure scissors with curved blades, and scissors with long points as necessary. A scalpel or small craft tool with a sharp blade is also useful for cutting out.

A roller is needed to flatten the collage shapes. Use a small wooden roller like those used for pressing wallpaper seams. Otherwise, use a small craft roller or a rolling pin.

Other materials required are a pencil, eraser, ruler, scrap paper.

Lily pond collage

This appealing picture is a good introduction to collage with its simple but appealing shapes. Copy our collage, or substitute a portrait of your own pet.

▽ *Water ripples, crazy paving, a cat, fish and water lilies are easy to create with paper collage.*

You will need
◇ White card for background
◇ Selection of papers
◇ Adhesive, roller
◇ Scissors, craft knife
◇ Drawing materials

1 Scale up the diagram to the required size and make a rough sketch to help you plan the colours and composition. Draw a border ⅝in (1.5cm) deep round the edge of the background card, to protect the finished collage. Mark in the crazy paving area.

2 Collect a selection of blue coloured papers for the water and tear these into narrow strips. Experiment by tearing the paper in different directions, both across and down a page. The white rough edges of the torn strips create the illusion of surface ripples.

3 Lay each blue strip wrong side up on a sheet of scrap paper (not newspaper which may leave marks on the paper strips) and spread with adhesive, or roll over with hot wax. Start sticking the strips at the top of the pond and, working downwards, slightly overlap each row of strips. Allow each strip to overlap the crazy paving edge.

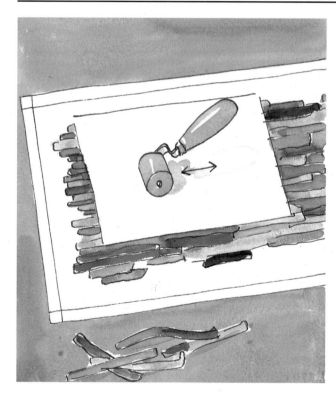

4 When the water area is complete, place a sheet of clean paper over the work and flatten the collage with a small roller.

5 Using two or more shades of green to create each leaf, cut out the lily leaves and reeds. Vary the colour and texture. Use a combination of plain papers and printed magazine pages to add visual interest. Stick in place, overlapping paving area slightly. Cut out orange-coloured fish shapes and stick these in position under leaves.

6 Cut out roughly shaped squares from selected colours to form the crazy paving. Stick squares round the pond edge first, then fill out the background, reaching into the drawn border. Flatten with roller as before.

7 Use light and dark lemon yellow papers to make the lily petals. Stick in place. Add centre details in orange. Cut and tear the paper shapes to make the cat. Blend the colours carefully to give the body a feeling of shape. Stick in place. Cut out more fish shapes and arrange them on the pond to balance the composition. Stick some extra blue strips over parts of the fish to give an impression of movement.

TIP ◆ DISPLAYING COLLAGES

Display collages behind glass to keep them clean and prevent paper shapes from shifting. Avoid hanging them near direct sources of heat, such as radiators, which can loosen the paper.

---

8 Place a sheet of paper over the entire collage and run the roller over the paper to help flatten out all the shapes. To protect the finished work, cover the border edge with a card mount and then place the picture in a frame.

1 square = 1⅜in (3.5cm)

CELEBRATE WITH PAPER

◇

◇

Pop up cards

*Everyone likes to receive a greetings card,
and a pop up card is a real bonus. However simple the image,
the ingenuity of the paper design is a source of
amusement. Pop up cards look quite complex, but many are
based on simple folds and cuts.*

△ *Say good luck with a black cat that sits on the mantelpiece, or send a
sweet message with a row of teddy bears crowding round the
honeypot. You can use the basic structures shown here to develop
your own designs for pop up cards.*

Design ideas

The 'pop ups' on pop up cards are usually worked by the simple process of opening the card. The pop up shape can be a separate piece of paper attached to each side of the centre fold, or it can be part of the card itself, achieved by folding and cutting the inside of the card so that an image jumps out as the card is opened. The cards shown here all work along the lines of the first simple technique which uses a glued-on paper shape.

Very often it is the really simple ideas which are the most effective. A pop up image which links directly with the message gives special impact, like the black cat with 'good luck', or a heart with 'I love you'. Unless you are confident with your drawing ability, use simple outline images or make up collages from printed papers for the pop ups. Outlines can be traced from magazines, or from children's picture books where the stylized drawings provide good subjects.

Suitable papers

Choose papers that are not too floppy, or so thick that they do not bend easily. Avoid papers which mark or crack, such as foils or coated papers like poster paper. Cartridge weight paper and artist's papers like Canson paper are good to work with because they fold easily and have a nice texture.

Some handmade or hand-coloured papers can be used too. Try out different pop up effects using typing or copy paper before cutting into your best paper.

Materials and equipment

Paper and card are the main materials. It is worth collecting all kinds of scraps, so that you have a good selection to choose from.

Adhesives Stick adhesive, which does not leave sticky trails, is clean and easy to use. Low tack spray adhesive, which is available from graphic supply shops, can also be used, and is particularly useful for sticking large areas and very small or fragile shapes that are difficult to handle.

Pens and pencils to write your message and draw in details, can be cartridge filled, ball or fibre point. Some of the unusual felt tip pens, like those with metallic ink or two colours, are most effective, and add a professional touch.

Use a soft lead pencil for marking fold lines and outlines.

A sharp craft knife is needed for cutting out the card shape and scoring fold lines.

A cutting edge like a metal ruler is needed to use with the craft knife.

Tracing paper is used for transferring the design and as a pattern.

Carbon paper is used for transferring the design from the tracing to the card.

A set square (triangle) and ruler for drawing out the card.

Sharp pointed scissors and manicure scissors are needed for cutting out the intricate shapes.

Tweezers are useful for handling small shapes.

The work surface should be protected with hardboard or card.

Cutting out cards

Most greetings cards are made by either folding a single sheet of paper in half, or folding a large sheet into four, so that the card is double thickness. The latter is useful when using fairly thin paper, as it gives the card more rigidity.

Before adding the details, cut the paper to the required size, using a set square and ruler for accuracy, and cutting out the outline with a craft knife.

Lightly mark in the fold lines and gently score along these, then fold the paper into its finished shape. Check that all the edges are level and even and trim to adjust the fit if necessary.

Making pop up cards

Once you have a design idea for a card, you must decide how to turn it into a reality. One of the simplest ways to make a pop up shape is to add a hinged inset which is folded in the opposite direction to the card, as in the honeybear card on the following page. Alternatively, you can add extra folds to the insert so that it hinges up as the card is opened.

Using the same basic paper cutting and folding techniques and a little imagination, you can adapt the ideas to suit any occasion.

▷ *This black cat, sitting smugly on a tiled floor, is a perfect way to send greetings to a cat lover, or to say 'Good luck'.*

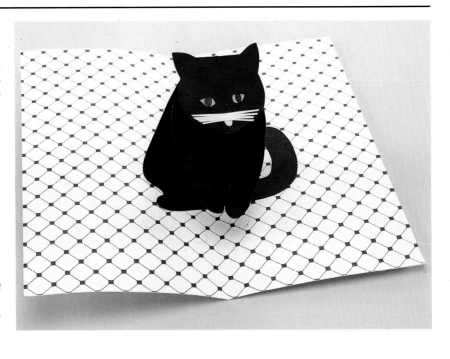

Black cat card

1 Fold and crease the white paper in half. Glue the tile paper and cover the inside of the card.

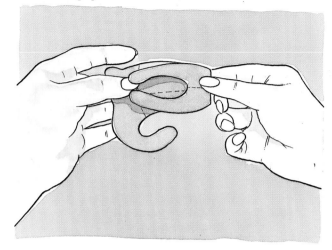

You will need
◇ Adhesive
◇ Craft knife and scissors
◇ Ruler and set square
◇ Cutting surface
◇ Tracing paper and carbon paper
◇ Coloured pens
◇ White paper measuring 9in (23cm) square
◇ Dolls' house floor tile paper 9in (23cm) square
◇ Black paper for cat
◇ Scraps of green, pink, white and black paper for eyes, tongue, whiskers and nose

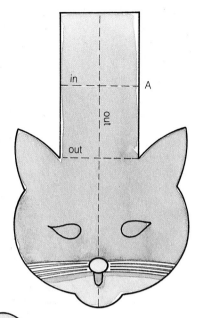

2 Trace the cat pattern pieces on to black paper, draw in fold lines and cut out. Crease all lines, starting at the centre, then folding the lower part of the body in towards the upper part, so that the cat 'sits'.

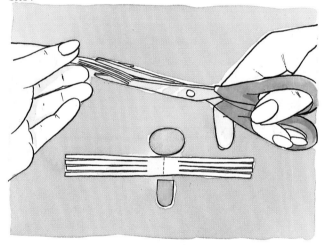

3 Cut out the facial features, following the outlines on the tracing, using tweezers to handle the shapes. To make the whiskers, fold a small strip of paper in half and make narrow snips almost to the centre. Trim to the depth of the nose, and glue the nose to the centre of the whiskers. Glue the tongue behind the whiskers, then glue the unit to the centre of the head. Trim the whiskers to width of face.

4 Glue the head to the body, matching up fold lines marked A. Gently re-crease the fold line.

5 Sit the cat in the centre of the card and gently close it. Place the cat so that its head does not protrude from the card. Mark its required position, about 3in (7.5cm) from the base and spread glue on the lower body and tail.

6 Press the cat into place and close the card gently. Add your message to the cover, or inside the card.

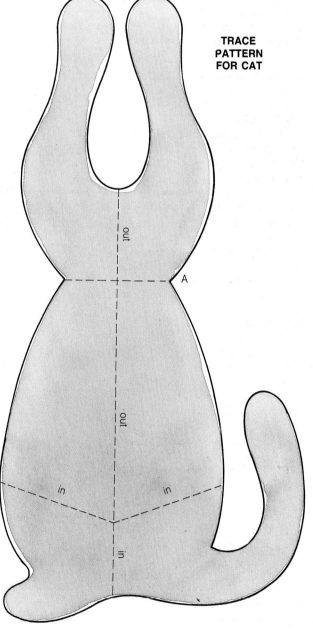

TRACE PATTERN FOR CAT

Honey bear card

1 To make the basic card, fold the brown paper in half lengthways, then in half widthways. Crease the fold lines sharply.

2 Trace six bear outlines on to yellow paper, trace another two so they face in the opposite direction. Stick four identical bears to the front of the card.

3 Using the tracing as a guide, draw in the eyes and noses, in black, and cut four different coloured bow ties. Stick in place.

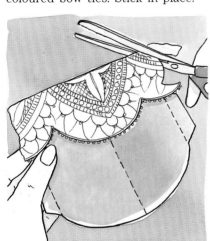

4 Cut out the honey pot shape and fold along crease lines. Cut a piece of doily a little wider and deeper than the pattern outline and stick this to the pot. Fold the excess to the back of the pot and cut the sides to shape as shown. Cut a label, add the word 'honey', and stick in place.

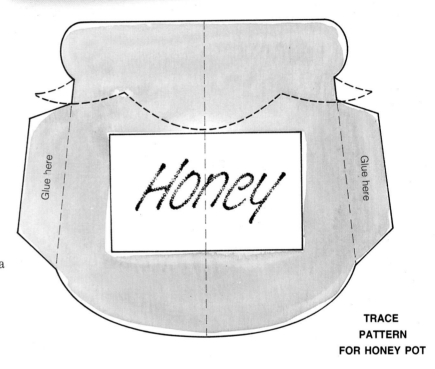

Glue here

Glue here

Honey

TRACE PATTERN FOR HONEY POT

Cut 6 facing this way, cut 2 facing opposite way

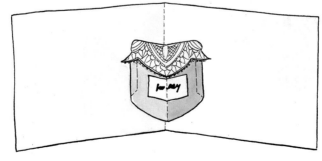

5 Open the card flat, and apply glue to the tabs. Position the honey pot so that the centre crease line is in line with the card centre fold and each tab fold line is 1⅜in (3.5cm) from the card centre at the top of the pot, and 1½in (4cm) at the base.

6 Stick the remaining bears in place on each side of the honey pot. Cut four more bow ties. Stick them in place and add the bears' features. Finally, add your message.

You will need
◇ Adhesive
◇ Craft knife and scissors
◇ Ruler and set square (triangle)
◇ Cutting surface
◇ Tracing paper and carbon paper
◇ Coloured pens
◇ Brown paper measuring 17¾in (45cm) long and 10in (25cm) high
◇ Yellow paper for bears
◇ Light brown paper for honey pot
◇ Paper doily and plain white paper
◇ Scraps of brightly coloured paper for bow ties and honey pot trim

Paper patch designs

Decorate greetings cards and cardboard boxes
with patchwork and woven designs made from scraps of wrapping
paper. By choosing scaled-down prints and planning
each design well, the paper can be worked like cloth to create
perfect miniature patchwork and woven patterns.

Small scale examples of familiar crafts like patchwork and weaving have a special appeal but can be fiddly to work. Similar effects are easier to achieve with paper, using simple shapes like triangles,

squares and rectangles. Traditional patchwork designs can be copied by piecing together random paper shapes, or by arranging the shapes in blocks, separated by criss-cross strips to build up formal designs.

▽ *Learn to hoard scraps of favourite wrapping papers — they can be used very effectively to decorate greeting cards. The mounts for the cards can be bought from craft and needlework stores.*

Patchwork inspired effects can also be achieved by weaving strips together to build up blocks and squares. This simplifies the handling of very small shapes, making the method ideal for working more intricate details.

See pages 93-96 for instructions about weaving paper.

Materials and equipment

Papers suitable for paper patch designs include giftwrap, foils, art papers and any paper that is fairly firm and handles well. Patterned papers should have small scale designs if details are to show up. Specialist papers like doll's house papers are also useful.

Cards specially designed with cut out 'windows' to hold your designs are available from craft shops and mail order specialists, as are small cardboard boxes.

Craft knife and **protective cutting surface** are used for cutting the papers. Use a knife with a fine blade and cut along a metal ruler.

Tweezers are useful for handling very small shapes.

Adhesives such as stock adhesives are simple and clean to use. Use sticky tape to hold the finished designs inside the card.

Other equipment required: ruler, pencil and scissors, tracing paper.

Working designs

Successful designs can be worked with as few as four to six papers or, if you prefer, lots of different papers. Look at patchwork and weaving patterns for ideas and simplify them if necessary. Remember that small scale designs require less detail. Use shiny papers to add interest as focal points or to use as borders on design.

Paper patch cards

All the designs shown on page 107 are set in ready-made window greetings cards and the designs are worked to fit each window shape.

The patchwork designs are put together on a background paper, which then forms an integral part of the design.

The woven designs are mounted on to a backing paper.

1 Make a tracing of the card window shape and transfer it lightly to the chosen background paper, to act as a design outline.

2 Make random designs by first cutting out a selection of triangles and patches with a craft knife. Spread adhesive over the paper and arrange the shapes on top, starting with larger shapes. Overlap and glue the pieces as required. Add colourful details and small shapes last.

3 Trim the finished design to size, ready to mount behind the window front. Place the design behind the window, adjust fit and hold with sticky tape on each side.

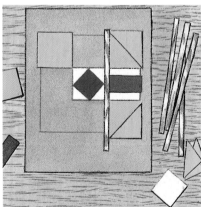

4 Formal designs are worked by either centring and gluing a patch on the background paper, or working in from the four corners, sticking each shape in place as required. Choose squares and triangles, overlayed with contrast strips for impact.

Weaving designs

These can be worked from warp and weft strips of an equal size or strips in a variety of sizes. Try out different effects. The designs can be mounted either vertically or horizontally behind each of the window frames.

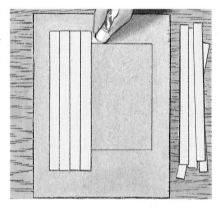

1 Start by cutting warp strips a little longer than the window shape and align them, side by side on a backing paper. Secure with adhesive along one end.

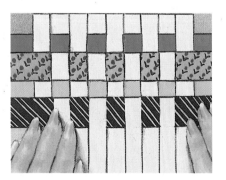

2 Cut weft strips slightly wider than required and thread them through the warp. Gently push the strips up against each other for a close fit. Finish the design, trim, and stick edges to the backing.

Quick 3D découpage

*Three dimensional pictures and greetings
cards are easy to make with giftwrap papers and self-
adhesive foam pads. Designs come alive when
motifs are cut from their background and rearranged in
raised layers on plain coloured card.*

This quick version of 3D découpage is ideal for creating original greetings cards and labels. As the motifs are cut from giftwrap papers it is possible to achieve impressive effects by co-ordinating the wrapping with a custom-made card. The technique can also be used to add another dimension to wall posters or paper friezes.

△ *The scale of the motifs used will determine the finished size of the card. Tiny motifs suit gift tags, but may need to be grouped on a larger greetings card. Large motifs can be used for a super-sized card.*

Materials and equipment

Papers Three to five motifs are needed for each 3D design so use giftwrap papers with repeated motifs. The motifs should have clearly defined outlines for visual impact, and to use as guides when cutting out. Strengthen giftwrap by backing it with typing or drawing paper before cutting out the motifs. Mount the finished designs on thin card which folds easily, or thick art papers. Pre-cut greetings card blanks, available from craft shops, can also be used.

Adhesives Use a spray adhesive to join backing paper to giftwrap and to stick the first motif to the background. Alternatively, use stick adhesive or clear craft glue.

Self-adhesive foam pads, available from stationery shops, are used to separate and lift the layers.

Scissors You need small, sharp-pointed scissors for cutting out the motifs. Use curved manicure scissors for intricate shapes.

Other materials needed are a craft knife, straight edge to cut against, ruler, set square, pencil. Use old papers to protect surfaces when using spray adhesive, or make a spray booth from a cardboard box.

3D greetings card

1 Cut out the motifs, leaving a generous margin all round. You will require four or five motifs, depending on how many details you wish to emphasize. Place the motifs in the spray booth or on a protected surface and spray the back of each with adhesive. Press on to typing or drawing paper.

2 Cut out two complete motifs, along design outline. Lay one on to background card/paper to see the effect and to plan finished card size. Mark out required measurement and decide if fold should be at side or top. Cut out. Gently score along fold line with a craft knife and bend to shape.

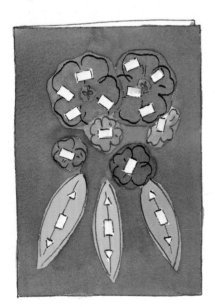

3 Spray the back of one motif with adhesive and position on card front. Cover motif with adhesive pads, cutting them into smaller pieces to fit motifs as necessary. Carefully place the second motif on top.

4 Cut out remaining motifs and discard more of the background with each one, so that final layer has only small details.

5 Stick the third layer in place with adhesive pads, positioning these as required under the cut details. Repeat with final layers.

Christmas cards

*Cut-out 'window' and silhouette designs
featuring familiar seasonal themes make eye-catching
additions to Christmas card displays. Make them
from brightly coloured card and giftwrap papers, to send
a special personal touch with your greetings.*

Choose stiff art papers or thin card to make the cards and use foils, white frosted paper and patterned giftwrap for the details. Cut out the designs using a small craft knife.

Use a metal ruler to rest against when cutting. Glue details with a stick adhesive suitable for paper. Scale up the designs and transfer them to tracing paper.

▽ *The striking outlines of a poinsettia, a festive wreath and a snow scene provide the inspiration for these colourful novelty Christmas cards.*

Window wreath
You will need
◇ Green card
◇ Red foil
◇ White frosted paper

1 Cut a card rectangle 12 x 8$^1/_8$in (30 x 20.3cm). Trace window design on right-hand side of card so fold line is at centre. Cut a rectangle of frosted paper 7$^1/_2$ x 5in (19 x 12.5cm).

2 Trace the ribbon trim for the wreath on to red foil and cut out. Stick in place on card.

3 Gently score along fold line to mark the card fold. Cut away all cut-out areas of the design. Cut along edge of left-hand side of window sill.

4 Fold card in half along scored line and cut away excess on the right side of window through both card thicknesses. Glue the rectangle of frosted paper behind the cut-out areas of the design. Trim if needed.

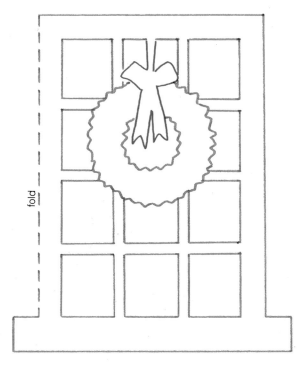

Snow scene
You will need
◇ Blue card
◇ White frosted paper
◇ Gold foil giftwrap
◇ Gold decoration

1 From card cut a rectangle 11 x 8$^1/_8$in (28 x 20.3cm). Trace and scale-up the snow scene and transfer it to the right-hand side, so the fold line is at the centre.

2 Score along fold line then cut away cut-out areas. Fold card in half along scored line and cut curved edge at the top of the card through both thicknesses.

3 Cut frosted paper to fit behind the two lower sections of the design, and glue in place round edges. Cut gold foil to fit top section and stick in place. Add more gold with motifs as shown in photograph.

Poinsettia
You will need
◇ Red card
◇ Gold foil giftwrap
◇ Tapestry needle

1 Cut a card rectangle 14$^5/_8$ x 6$^1/_4$in (37.3 x 16cm). Draw the poinsettia on the lower section, so the fold line is positioned horizontally across the centre.

2 Score along the fold lines, then cut along the petal outlines that are above the scored line. Fold the card along the scored line and cut away all the cut-outs through both thicknesses.

3 Open out the card and pierce small holes through the centre of each flower with the needle. Trace the bow trim for the flowerpot on to gold foil giftwrap and cut out. Stick in place. Highlight the flower petals with small snips of gold.

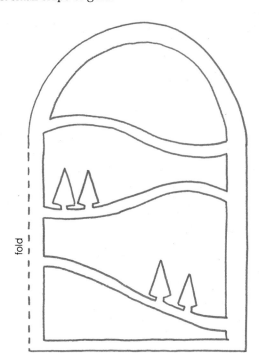

Gift wrapping

A well-wrapped present is a pleasure to receive,
but often rather daunting to achieve. You can produce eye-catching
wrapping that will not take an age to create, with
simple decorations. Follow these ideas to bring your own flair
and add something special to gift wrapping.

Wrapping presents should be a pleasure, but often the final effort of presenting the gift poses a problem. Giftwrap packs of matching papers and ready-made bows are readily available, but sometimes adding your own special style to a gift is a much more attractive option. The difficulty is how and where to begin.

Papers and trims

Giftwrap papers are not the only papers that can be used to make attractive wrappings for presents. Art papers, tissue papers, foils, wallpapers and even newspapers can all look good, either used on their own, or combined with other papers. The trims used on presents are important finishing touches, and these can be gathered from a variety of sources. It is worth building up a collection of useful materials to keep at hand.

Stationery suppliers stock coloured labels, and self-adhesive stickers, such as stars and coloured spots, which are useful for building up patterns, or adding details. Paper doilies and tableware, and craft accessories like compressed balls can all be useful. Seasonal decorations, plastic flowers and foliage can be transformed too, by spraying them a new colour.

Box shapes

If you are faced with an impossibly lumpy or awkwardly shaped gift, the easiest way to wrap it is to put it in a box, as box shapes are the easiest to cover. The paper looks good, with neatly folded corners, and the gift is not likely to burst through its wrappings.

▷ *Brightly coloured wrappings, ribbons and decorations make an exciting starting point for wrapping a special present.*

114

How to wrap a box

Whether the box is rectangular or square, the method for wrapping it is the same. Neat and evenly folded edges and corners are easy to achieve; avoid problems by always using the right amount of paper; the tendency is to use a whole sheet of paper when much less is sufficient.

1 Lay the box on a sheet of paper and wrap it round the box. Mark an overlap of 4in (10cm) (less for small gifts) and cut the paper to this size. The width should be sufficient to wrap two thirds of the way up each side of the box. Trim the paper to fit.

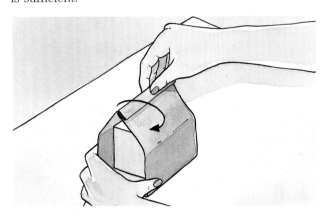

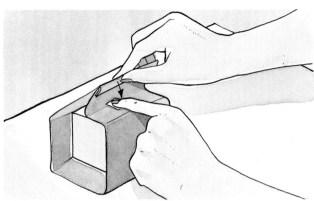

2 Replace the box in the centre of the paper, and wrap the paper round. Hold the two edges level at the top of the box, and fold them over together. Pinch the fold, ¾in (2cm) below the edges, (less for smaller boxes) and run fingers and thumbs along the fold to make a crisp straight line.

3 Fold the paper down on to the box, moving the entire wrapping slightly, so that the fold line is centred on the box. Hold with a piece of double sided sticky tape attached under the fold.

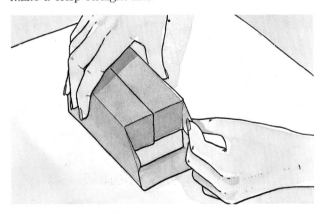

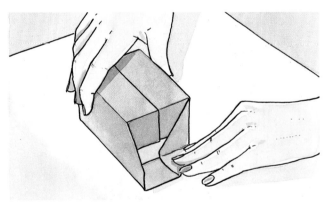

4 Check that the box is centred in the wrapping. At one end, press down the folded edge so it is flat against the end of the box. Crease the two resulting side folds.

5 Push in one side fold so it is flat against the end of the box and crease the resulting lower fold with your fingers.

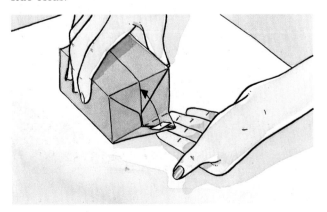

6 Push in the other side fold and crease it as before. Fold up the resulting triangular flap and attach it to the end of the box with double sided sticky tape attached across all the triangle folds. Repeat for the other end of the box.

◆ TIP   DOUBLE PLEATED FOLD

This style of folded overlap is a slight variation of the style described above. It looks particularly attractive used as a finish on plain wrapping paper. Allow twice the usual amount for the overlap and pinch the edges together as before.

Take a large tuck, 2in (5cm) deep, and fold this over as described in step 2 above, then fold it back on itself to form a raised panel about 1in (2.5cm) wide down the centre of the package. Adjust the position of the paper so that the folded panel is centred, and finish wrapping the ends as before.

DESIGN IDEAS

Fans

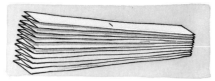

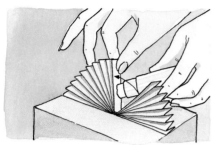

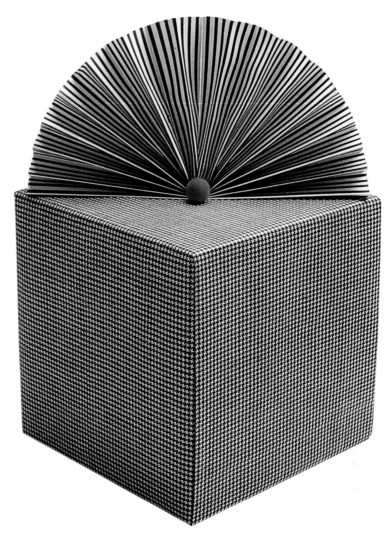

To make a fan to cover the width of the box, take the measurement across the top of the lid. This will be the width of the paper strip used to make the fan. The longer the paper strip, the fuller the fan will be. Mark the centre of the paper width, and pleat the paper in concertina folds. Fold the pleats in half, and run a line of glue along one end pleat. Position this so it matches the adjacent pleat exactly, so the join is not noticeable. Try the fan for fit and cut away some of the pleats if the effect is too full. Glue the fan in place.

Folded ribbon bows

These can be made from giftwrap ribbon, or strips cut from matching or contrasting wrapping papers. Cut eight or more strips to the required width and length, and fold them, without creasing, so the ends overlap. Glue the overlap to form loops, then put a dab of glue in the centre of the band, or secure with double sided sticky tape. Stick the bands across each other, criss cross fashion, to form a pompon bow.

Bow ties

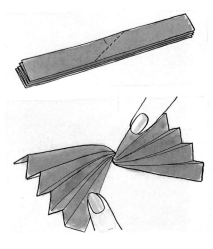

These can be made from any size paper strip, or from two contrasting papers pleated together as one. Pleat the paper crisply with an average of eight to ten narrow folds, and pinch the pleated strip together in the middle. Mark the centre point. Draw a line diagonally across the centre, and fold the pleats along this line. Pull the pleats on the left side over towards you and glue the underside of the end pleat to the top of the box. Glue the underside of the diagonal end pleat in place and repeat with the other pleats.

△ *Gold has a dramatic effect when used to decorate a special gift. Spray plastic fruits and leaves (Christmas decorations are ideal) with a multi-purpose gold paint. Glue them to the top of the package using a clear adhesive, and team them with a richly textured wrapping paper.*

△ *Ready-made folded paper fruit and flower decorations are used to add an exotic touch to a simply wrapped gift box. Cocktail parasols would be a good alternative to flowers, or sections taken from folded Christmas streamers. Secure to the box with clear adhesive or double sided sticky tape.*

Gift bags

*Paper tote bags are versatile containers and the ideal
gift wrap solution for awkward shapes. They can be made in a
variety of sizes, from almost any paper you choose.
Pretty enough to keep and use as attractive lightweight holdalls
for knitting or embroidery materials.*

Design ideas

The contents themselves often suggest a decorative finish. A plain tote bag would contrast with a brightly patterned scarf or piece of china, or a leafy design could cover a difficult-to-wrap houseplant.

Tote bags can be made into gifts in themselves; many children would love a tote filled with sweets, then tied with edible liquorice ribbons, or a bag which sported handles made from brightly coloured shoe laces or hair ornaments.

Very often the design on the paper will suggest a style for the smaller accompanying details, such as whether handles would look best in cord or ribbon, or the shape and colour for a gift tag.

Gift bag sizes

The proportions of a tote bag are usually determined by the size of the contents you wish to wrap. The pattern overleaf can be adapted to make a tall bag, or a mini bag.

Measure the depth, width and height of the article to be wrapped. The bag dimensions must be larger than these measurements, to allow for any protective wrapping such as tissue paper.

Whatever size tote bag you choose to make, the depth of the main overlap sections at the base of the tote should always measure more than half the depth of each tote side (marked on the pattern 'a+½ again'). This ensures a good size overlap that can be stuck securely to provide a firm base and strengthen the bag. All 'a' measurements should be equal, so that the tote bag can fold flat.

Materials and equipment
Paper

It is important to choose papers that handle well and do not crack, or lose their surface colour or sheen when folded.

Gift wrapping paper is an obvious choice as it is readily available in so many pattern and colour variations. It is a good idea to stiffen the paper with wall lining paper, as described in the instructions overleaf.

Wallpaper is strong, and comes in good sized pieces.

Other paper such as handmade papers, art papers and newspapers· (so long as they are strong enough) can be used to make distinctive tote bags. Foils look attractive, but some mark rather easily, so if you want to use these it is wise to test them before you start.

Adhesive

The type which comes in a stick is the most convenient to use and gives excellent results.

Cutting and folding equipment

You will also need a sharp pencil for marking out cutting and fold lines, a ruler, set square and sharp scissors or craft knife and metal ruler. If you use a craft knife for cutting you will need a firm surface — a large sheet of card or hardboard is ideal.

A hole punch is also necessary for making holes for the handles.

Handling paper
Cutting paper

For a clean, accurate outline use scissors or cut with a craft knife held against a metal cutting edge.

The work should be laid on a flat, protective surface such as a cutting mat or spare piece of wood.

Folding paper
To make a crisp fold hold a ruler along the marked line and lightly run the back of the scissors along the ruler. Carefully fold the paper against the ruler to give a crisp, clean line.

With heavier paper and card use a craft knife held against a metal ruler to score the surface lightly before folding it. This gives greater accuracy, but care should be taken that you do not cut through the surface.

Joining sheets of paper

If you need to join sheets to make a large bag, overlap one edge by ½in (1.2cm), then glue the overlap flat using an adhesive stick. When you draw the tote bag shape on to the paper, place one of the vertical pattern lines on the edge of the join. This allows the paper tote to fold easily.

Making a gift bag

The pattern below is the outline shape required for the paper lining used to strengthen the tote bag. Adjust the proportions, then cut out the lining and make the necessary folds and creases before sticking it to the back of the cover paper. If your paper is strong enough not to need a lining, the pattern can be drawn directly on to the back. In this case you should allow an extra 2½in (6.5cm) above the top edge for turnings.

Extra support can be given to the handles by gluing a reinforcing strip of thin card along this top edge. As an added measure, card inserts can also be placed in the base of the bag to give extra strength and rigidity.

You will need
◇ Decorative paper
◇ Cartridge paper (drawing paper)
◇ Thin card (illustration or poster board)
◇ Adhesive stick
◇ Scissors or craft knife
◇ Cutting surface
◇ Ruler
◇ Set square (triangle)
◇ Cord or ribbon
◇ Hole punch

1 Lay the cartridge paper flat, then using a ruler and set square, mark out the measurements for your tote bag following the diagram below. Cut out.

2 Starting with the main vertical lines, crease the folds in the directions shown. Crease the base line, and the line running across the back section.

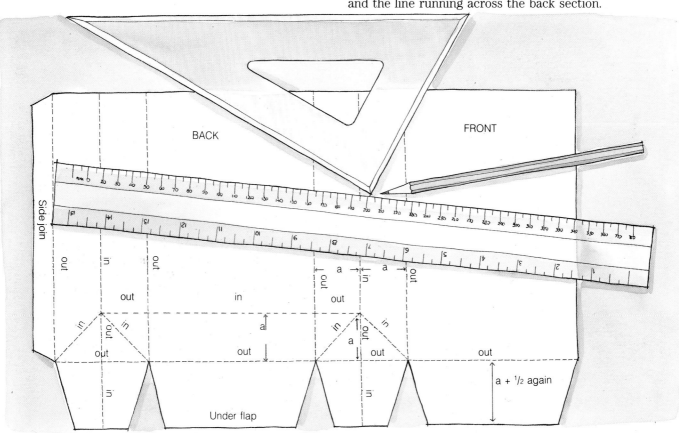

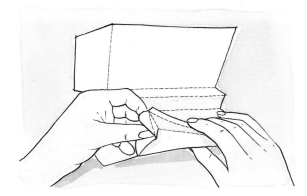

3 Crease the triangular shapes on the side sections by first running the scissors or knife along the lines. Next, fold the side lines together, and pinch the triangles into place.

4 Lay the cartridge paper flat, drawn line side facing up. Spread adhesive along edges and fold lines. Cut out the cover paper — make sure it is at least ¾in (2cm) larger all round, with at least 2½in (6cm) overlap at the top. Lay the cover paper flat, wrong side up, and lay the paper lining on to this, sticky side down, allowing for space for the overlap.

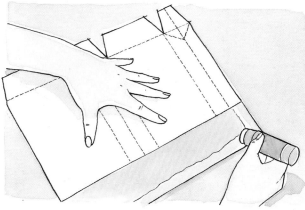

5 Smooth the paper in place, then trim around the edge of the cartridge paper, leaving the overlap free. Run a line of adhesive along the top and sides of the overlap paper, fold it over and smooth it in place. Check papers are firmly stuck at edges, then gently press the creases into the paper again.

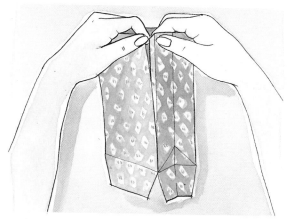

6 Spread adhesive along the side join flap and place it under the tote front. Carefully align the top edge, sides and base fold line.

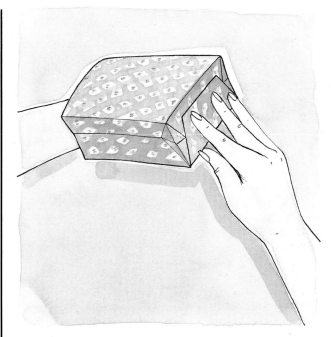

7 Turn the bag upside down. Spread adhesive on the edges of the right sides of the side flaps, and along the edge of the wrong side of the under flap. With one hand inside the bag, press the flaps together, making sure the tote keeps its shape. Stick down base flap and press firmly in place.

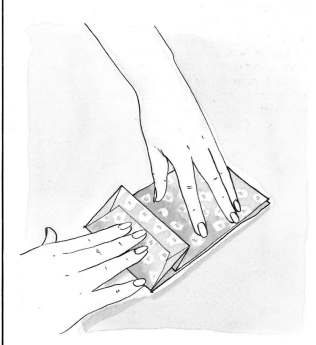

8 Smooth the tote bag edges making sure they all line up. Gently press the base section flat, so that it folds to the back of the bag.

9 The position of the handles will depend on the size and proportion of your bag. It will also depend on how far your hole punch will reach over the top edge of the bag. A good guide is to mark the holes between a third to a quarter of the front width in from each side.

10 For each handle, cut a length of cord or ribbon long enough to thread through both holes to make a comfortable handle, with enough over to knot on the wrong side.

Different handles and ties

△ Simple cord handles are practical and can be contrasted or colour matched to the tote bag. They can be knotted in a loop on the inside as here.

△ Thread two shades of ribbon together to make a feature on a plain tote bag. Punch holes in the sides, too, so the ribbons gather the bag closed.

△ Ribbon handles can be threaded from the wrong side, passed through beads and knotted to make a practical and decorative finishing touch.

△ Prettily edged ribbons can make extravagant looking ties. Thread two lengths of ribbon through from the front to the back of the bag and tie in bows.

Gift tags

Customize your tote bags with matching card ties. Use the paper pattern as a starting point for designs and keep them simple for the best effect. Use an adhesive stick to mount the paper on to thin card or cartridge paper, carefully score a fold line if required and cut out through all layers. Use a hole punch and toning thread or ribbon for a professional looking finish.

Papers with motifs such as flowers make good subjects for gift tags. Carefully cut out the pattern and mount it on a plain background. Stick this to card and cut out with small pointed scissors. Tags shaped as mini totes are fun — use a compass or coin to help draw the handle curve. Make a paper pattern so that you can make several tags. Use a compass, too, for hearts. Draw the pattern on folded paper so both sides are equal before cutting out the heart.

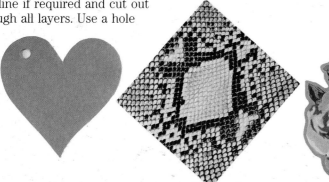

Flat-pack boxes

*Lightweight flat-pack boxes are ideal
containers for fragile gifts or awkwardly shaped presents.
The boxes look smart and can be tailor-made to suit
the contents. Paper is used to cover the basic box which can
then be decorated as you wish.*

Both styles of box shown here are easy to make and can be varied simply by changing the size and scale or the design treatment on each one. Miniature boxes are perfect for holding tiny gifts like jewellery, or for presenting one or two really special chocolates. Larger boxes are a good solution to the problem of wrapping several gifts at once, and for covering difficult to wrap objects.

One box is a basic cube with four overlapping shapes to form the lid. The sides can be lengthened, or the square enlarged or decreased as desired. The flatter box, with the elipse closures at each end, can be lengthened or widened, and is ideal for holding gifts like pens and pencils, ties, belts and scarves.

Materials and equipment

Thin card available from art shops and graphic suppliers is used to make the boxes. This should be roughly twice the thickness of cartridge paper so it is firm but soft enough for scissors to cut curves, and should fold easily without crumpling. Coloured card can be used but check that the colour does not crack when the card is scored with a knife.

Papers to cover the card can be giftwrap, thin wallpapers or art papers. Other paper can be used if it is strong enough to withstand adhesives and handles well. Some types of shiny paper and foil should be avoided as they tend to mark easily. Tracing paper, carbon paper and graph paper are used for transferring and changing the sizes of the boxes.

Adhesive such as spray adhesive sold in art and graphic shops for mounting work is the easiest and quickest way of sticking paper to card. Stick adhesive can be used for small boxes, but is hard to apply evenly on larger shapes.

Making the boxes

The most economical way to use card and paper is to make a number of boxes in various sizes. You'll find you can make several boxes from a single sheet of card and paper.

You will need

◇ Thin card (card stock, poster board or illustration board)
◇ Giftwrap paper
◇ Tracing paper and carbon paper (optional)
◇ Ruler, set square (triangle) and compass
◇ Pencil and eraser
◇ Spray adhesive
◇ Craft knife, cutting edge and cutting surface
◇ Scissors
◇ Glue or double-sided sticky tape

Transferring the designs

The box shapes can be drawn directly on to card or transferred as described: Take a tracing of the box and transfer to graph paper. Scale up or down by copying the shapes on to a larger or smaller grid as required then take a tracing of the finished box shape. Alternatively, enlarge or reduce your pattern on a photo copying machine.

Check that the paper used to cover the card is dense enough to hide the lines made by carbon paper. If you are using a light coloured paper it is advisable to draw the shape directly on to the card so that the pencil lines can be erased before covering the card with paper.

Box with end flaps

This box shape is ideal for gifts like scarves. It can be changed as desired. The ideal elipse size should not be too deep as this could strain the side join and distort the box. Note the position of the compass points on our diagram, and the proportions of elipse to box size if changing the shape of your particular box.

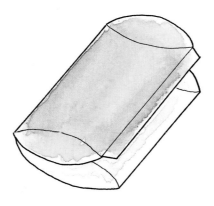

1 Draw the box shape on to card and cut out. Gently score along the elipse lines and fold lines. Ease the box to shape.

2 Follow instructions for spraying adhesive on card and sticking and cutting out paper as described in steps 3, 4 and 5 of 'box with overlap lid' on page 124.

3 Run adhesive or double sided sticky tape along the side overlap, and line up with side. Press firmly together. When completely dry, push in end flaps.

4 To open box, gently squeeze sides so that the flaps can be lifted easily. Add bows or other decorative trims as desired.

These slimline boxes are ideal for presenting small gifts. Their shape makes them ideal for popping in the post.

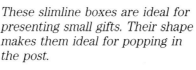

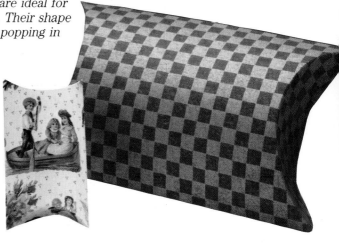

You will also need: a set square (triangle), ruler, compass and HB pencil for marking the box shape on to card. A craft knife, metal ruler as a cutting edge and cutting mat or protective surface for scoring the card. Scissors for cutting out the curves, glue or double-sided sticky tape for sticking the flaps.

Making a spray booth

When using spray adhesive it is important to prevent the fine sticky spray from settling on other surfaces, so it is necessary to use the spray in a confined area. A cardboard box large enough to take the flat cut-out box shape makes an ideal spray booth. Place the box on its side on some sheets of news-

paper and use more paper to protect any surrounding furnishings. Open the box lid flaps wide and place the card shape as far inside the box as possible. To spray, hold the can close to the inside of the box and spray using a sweeping motion. Handle the sticky card as little as possible when transferring it to the work surface.

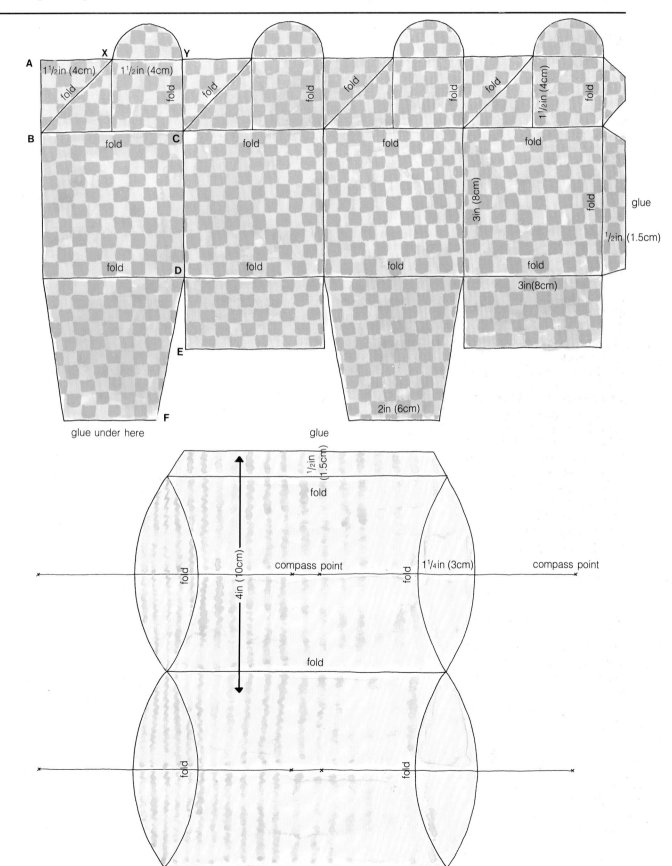

Box with overlap lid

Based on a square, the box can be any size, as long as each side is the same width. The distance between A and B should always be half the size of the distance between B and C. Likewise, the distance between D and E should be the same as A and B, and the distance between D and F should be the same as between B and C. To draw the half circles which make the lid overlaps, set the compass in the centre of line marked X and Y and draw between the two points. By following these proportions the overall size can change.

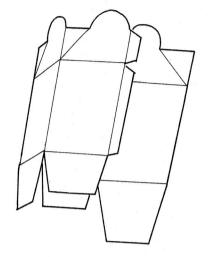

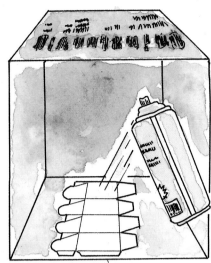

1 Draw or trace the box shape on to card, and cut out along the straight lines using a craft knife and cutting edge. Cut out the curves with scissors.

2 Gently score along all the fold lines and bend the lines to shape. Erase any pencil lines as required.

3 Place the box flat in the spraying booth, scored side upwards, and spray card evenly and thoroughly.

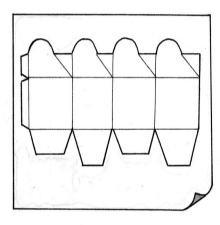

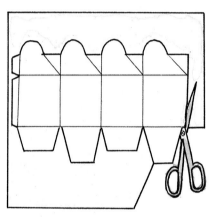

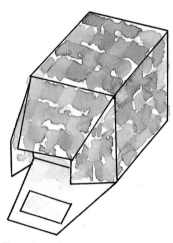

4 Lay giftwrap, wrong side facing on work top, and place sticky side of card over this. Take care to line up any obvious directional lines or pattern motifs with the card as desired. Smooth the card down firmly.

5 Turn card over and smooth paper flat, paying attention to edges of card. When dry cut out round the edge of the card, and check that all edges are stuck together. If necessary add a little glue to secure layers.

6 Ease box into shape. Run glue or double-sided tape along the side flaps. Press in position. Fold in base flaps, shortest first, and stick one large flap over other flap with glue or tape.

7 To close box, gently push top sections together, and push flat.

Casket gift boxes

*These presentation gift boxes are
designed to be seen open so their contents are on display.
The double shell structure provides a
deep lip edge and ready-made lining, to show striking
covering papers to full advantage.*

Each box shown here was made in one piece from a single sheet of giftwrap paper and a sheet of thin card. The lids can be sealed with a sticky fastener, or held closed with a variety of colourful ribbons, strings and ties.

Different effects are easy to achieve — take the paper design or the intended contents of the box as a starting point and add a variety of trims to complement, letting your imagination be your guide.

Materials and equipment

Papers Choose good quality giftwrap papers with surfaces which do not crack or mark easily. Glossy papers with a design printed on a light coloured background would work particularly well. Take care if choosing dark colour prints,

as the colours can scuff easily and spoil the effect.

Card Choose thin card (sold by the sheet in art shops and graphic suppliers) which can be cut easily with scissors. For a professional finish match the shade of the card with the main shade of the covering paper, as the card edges show on the corners of the boxes.

Adhesives Use a clear quick-drying craft glue for assembling the box. Laminate the paper to the card with a spray adhesive. For details on using this adhesive and how to protect surrounding surfaces see pages 123-124.

Craft knife and **scissors** Cut out the main box shape with a sharp craft knife or scalpel against a straight edge and use small pointed scissors to cut curves.

You will also need a protective surface to cut against when using a craft knife, a set square and metal ruler, pencil, eraser, tracing paper and sticky tape.

Making a casket box

You can make the boxes any size you like, but to fit the shape on to readily available card and giftwrap paper, you should scale up the diagram so that the box base measurement does not exceed 6 x 3³⁄₄in (15 x 9.6cm).

Scale up the diagram and transfer the shape to a large sheet of paper. Use this as a pattern for making a number of boxes.

Check all measurements are accurate and, if possible, use a set square to check that the right angles are correct.

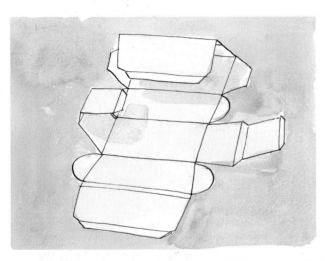

1 Trace the box shape on to card and lightly score all the fold lines. Cut out round the outline and bend the box into shape along the folds. Open out flat. Erase any pencil marks as these may show through light coloured papers.

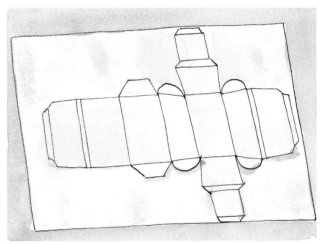

2 Protect work surface from spray adhesive. Lay sheet of giftwrap wrong side up on a flat surface. Spray scored side of card box shape thoroughly with adhesive. Lay the box sticky side down, on to the back of giftwrap and smooth flat.

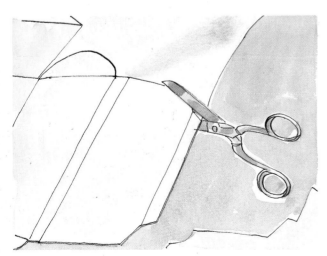

3 Turn the paper over and continue smoothing it flat. Turn work over again and, using a craft knife and scissors, carefully cut paper away around box outline. Gently crease along scorelines.

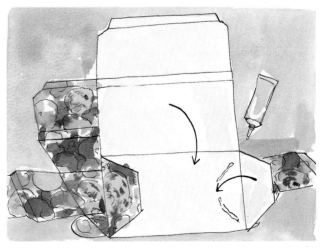

4 Spread a little glue on the underside of the lid side flaps and press to lid. Spread glue on the other side of the flaps and along underside of lid lining and press lining flat to lid. Leave to dry.

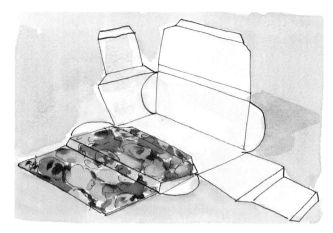

5 Working on one side of the box, spread glue on the paper sides of the curved side flaps. Press the box side up over the glued flaps, aligning the box corners and edges accurately. Repeat on the other side of the box, again taking care to align edges.

6 Fold the front lip edge to shape and run a line of glue under the front lining flap. Push the lining down into the box and press the glued flap to the base, pushing it back so that the fold aligns with the front inside edge of the box.

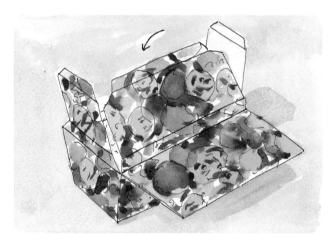

7 Re-crease the back lip edge and run a line of glue under the lining flap. Push the back lip edge into the box and align it with the base, in the same way as for the front.

8 Run a line of glue under the flap on a side lining and under the mitred corner of the lip edge. Fold the lining into the box and align as before. Press the mitred overlap in place and hold to stick, checking that all corners are at right angles. Repeat for other side.

9 Cut a rectangle of card to fit into the base of the box. This must be a little smaller than the actual base, so that it can be eased into place. Use spray adhesive to cover base lining with giftwrap. Add a little glue under the centre of the base lining and push it into the box.

10 The box is now ready to trim. Attach a sticky fastener to seal lid if required, or simply tie the box with ribbons, string or cord.

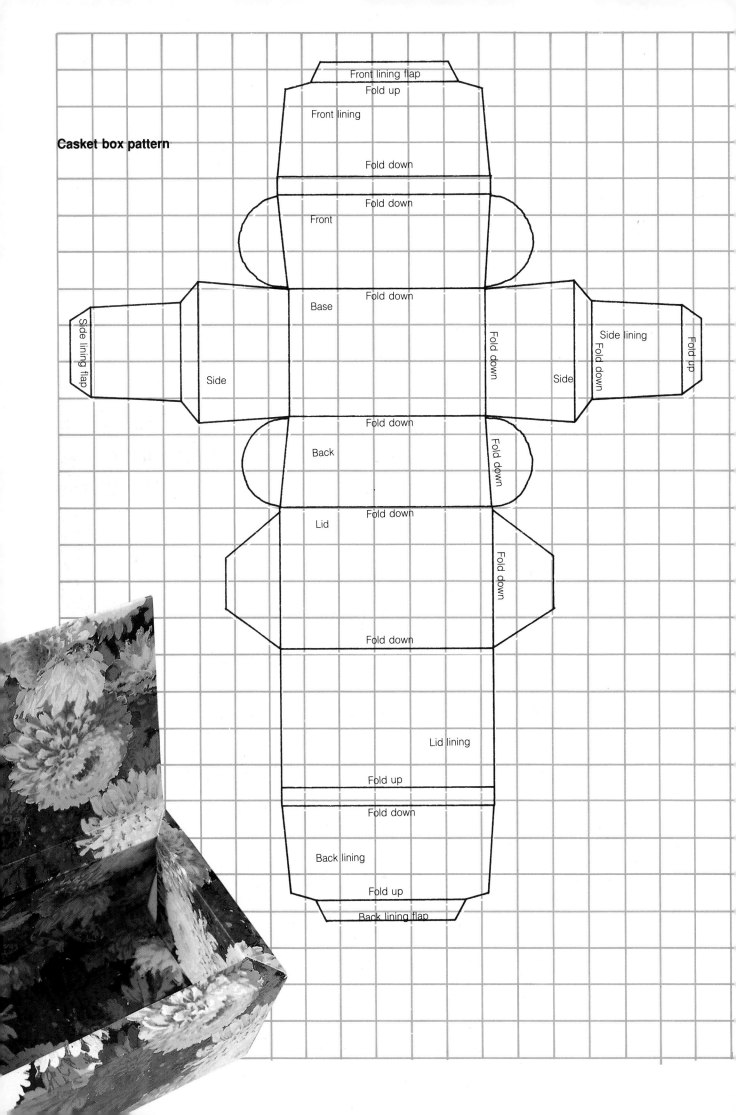

Casket box pattern

Front lining flap
Fold up
Front lining
Fold down
Fold down
Front
Fold down
Base
Side lining flap
Side
Fold down
Fold down
Side
Side lining
Fold up
Fold down
Back
Fold down
Fold down
Lid
Fold down
Lid lining
Fold up
Fold down
Back lining
Fold up
Back lining flap

Quilling flowers

*Quilled daisies and tiny carnations can
be made from fringed paper coils. Both designs are a
variation of the basic tight peg coil. Use
the flowers to decorate greetings cards and labels, or add
stems and arrange them as miniature bouquets.*

Vary the appearance of quilled daisies and carnations by making them from different sized paper strips and by colouring the petal edges. Use the proper quilling paper strips or cut the strips from wallpaper, giftwrap and glossy magazine pages for unusual effects.

You will need
◇ Strips of 9mm wide quilling paper
◇ Strips of 3mm wide quilling paper
◇ Sharp scissors with straight blades
◇ Quilling tool
◇ PVA adhesive (white glue)
◇ Cocktail stick
◇ Assorted felt tip pens (optional)

Daisies

1 Using a quarter of a length of the wider quilling paper, cut slits close together into the long edge, to within ¹/₈in (2mm) of the opposite straight edge. This gives the finished flower flexibility.

2 Glue the end of the narrower quilling paper to the uncut long edge. Use a tiny amount of PVA glue and spread with the tip of a cocktail stick. Leave to dry.

3 Roll all the fringed strip tightly in the quilling tool. Secure the loose end with glue and remove from the tool. Leave to dry. To complete the daisy, hold the base between finger and thumb, and brush the petals back with the thumb of the other hand.

Colour variations

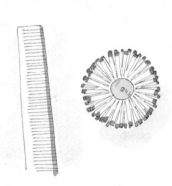

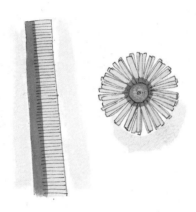

For petals with a tinted edge, colour the cut edges of the fringed strip with the tip of a felt tip pen, pastels or watercolour paints.

To produce a ring of colour round the flower centre, colour the lower edge of the fringed strip with a deeper band of colour.

For a three-colour effect, glue 2in (5cm) length of fringed contrast colour 6mm wide strip between the 3mm centre paper and outer petals.

Carnations

To make bigger flowers with fuller petals, double the length of the paper strip each time the paper width is doubled. Roll outer petal strips from fringed paper strips ³/₄in (2cm) or 1in (2.5cm) wide.

Make carnations by rolling a strip of fringed, 9mm wide paper. For bigger carnations, double the strip width and length as desired. The petal edges can be tinted in the same way as the daisies.

Making gift tags

Cut circles or other shapes from strong paper and attach a flower head with a dab of glue. Add a stem cut from narrow quilling paper and make leaves.

Making a bouquet

Instead of using individual flowers to trim a card, make a bouquet of flowers. To do this, make a number of flower heads and glue the underside of each centre to a florists' wire. If desired, add leaves to hide the join. Pinch all the stems together and wrap them with coloured tissue paper. Secure the bouquet with a pretty ribbon, tied in a bow. The bouquet could be used to trim stationery or gifts.

Christmas wreaths

*Wreaths of winter greenery celebrate
the festive season with rich mixtures of glossy foliage, fruits
and shiny berries. With versatile paper you can
copy nature to create realistic, everlasting wreaths or cheery
colourful designs, unmistakably made from paper.*

Seasonal decorations made of paper, especially wreaths, can look wonderfully festive. The wide range of papers and paper products gives inspiration and plenty of scope to

create all kinds of different effects. Our designs for wreaths use natural winter colours, but these can be changed to create fantasy designs in shimmery metallic papers.

▽ *A vine wreath, available from garden centres, forms the base for this dramatic design. The Christmas roses and leaves are made from plain and textured papers.*

Materials and equipment

Wreaths Florists' suppliers and garden centres sell wreaths made from twisted vines, cane, rush or grasses. Any of these can be used as a base for the decorations.

Papers Crêpe papers, artists' papers, twisted paper ribbon and tissue papers are ideal for decorating wreaths.

Florists' materials Stretchy coloured tape (gutta tape) for binding stems is needed to make naturalistic wreaths. Stamens — both berry and flower-centre types — add an authentic look to designs. Stem wires are used for strengthening and shaping leaves, and thin binding wire secures the trims.

Other materials include sharp scissors, craft knife, cutting edge, tracing paper.

Christmas rose wreath

The design copies the rich green shades of winter foliage with an arrangement of holly, trailing ivy leaves, Christmas roses (*Helleborus niger*) and imaginary nutty shapes, similar to hazelnuts. Tendrils soften and add interest to the shape of the wreath and gold glints emphasize the festive look.

You will need

◇ 10in (25cm) brown twisted vine/wicker wreath
◇ Double crêpe paper, white for roses, green for nuts
◇ Green paper ribbon for ivy leaves
◇ Green Canson paper for holly leaves
◇ Yellow tissue paper scraps
◇ Cotton wool scraps
◇ Large felt tip marker pens in gold and two shades of green
◇ Medium felt tip marker pens in brown and yellow
◇ Pale green crayon or oil pastel
◇ Eight ⅝in (1.5cm) diameter compressed paper balls for nuts
◇ Long pale yellow flower stamens
◇ Twelve red holly berry stamens
◇ Flower binding tape in green, brown, white
◇ Stem wires in green, white
◇ Spool of thin binding wire
◇ Clear, quick-drying craft glue
◇ Artists' acrylic fixative spray
◇ Large and small knitting needles
◇ Cord for hanging loop

Preparing the wreath

1 Highlight the bare wreath with the gold marker pen by drawing at random along some stems. Tie a loop of cord to back of wreath at centre top to hang it. Place loop so it does not show from front.

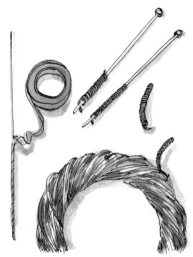

2 To make each tendril, wrap a stem wire diagonally with brown flower tape. Wind taped wire round a knitting needle and push coils together. Ease finished coil from the needle and twist tendril end round a wreath stem to secure. Make 10-12 tendrils in two sizes, and position evenly around the wreath. Adjust to desired shape after adding leaves and flowers.

Ivy leaves

1 Make templates from patterns on page 134. To make each leaf, cut a length of paper ribbon double required length of leaf. Spread glue evenly over one half, and lay half a flower-stem wire centrally along glued area. Fold paper over and press to stick.

2 Fold paper in half lengthways along wire and cut out leaf using template as a guide. Make at least 27 leaves. To colour each leaf, rub over with green felt tip pen, allowing some of the paper to show through around the edge of the leaf shape, then rub over with gold. Smudge to blend colours. Lightly spray leaves with fixative to give a slight gloss.

3 Wrap green stem tape diagonally round leaf wires. Starting with the smallest leaves, twist three stems together. Gradually twist in more leaf stems, placing them alternately as shown, so that the different wires form a main stem. Continue adding leaves to make a short spray of 12 leaves, then repeat method to make a spray of 15 leaves. Twist leaves to overlap one another in a naturalistic way.

4 Make a second spray. Position the two ivy sprays on each side of wreath so leaves point down. Push stem ends into the wreath and twist round to anchor. Use green stem wire to secure the main stems at points along wreath.

Holly leaves

1 Trace 12 holly leaf shapes on to Canson paper and cut out. Colour along the length of each leaf with green felt tip pen. Spray with fixative to give a sheen.

2 Gently score centre back of each leaf and fold to shape. Spread glue on half a green stem wire to same length as leaf. Align with edge of fold. Press in place.

3 Wire four leaves together, right sides facing. Twist four holly berries together and dab with gold pen. Place berries in centre of leaves. Wire to stems.

Nuts

1 To make each nut, glue a piece of stem wire into a compressed paper ball. Wrap paper ball with a square of green crêpe paper and secure to stem with binding wire.

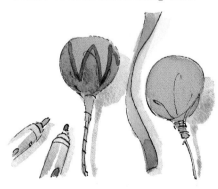

2 Use brown and green felt tip pens to draw tight leaf shapes over nut as shown. Highlight tops with gold spots. Bind stems diagonally with brown flower tape.

3 Using leaf pattern as a guide, cut out a fringe of green crêpe paper. Stretch crêpe over scissor blades to curve. With curves facing inwards, spread glue along the uncut section. Wrap round nut, positioning fringe just above nut base. Wrap rest with brown tape, and continue down stem as before.

4 Push the nuts into the wreath as far up the stems as possible, twisting stems to secure. Place four nuts on each side, so they are just visible amongst the ivy leaves, emerging below the smaller leaves and bend into a natural shape.

Christmas roses

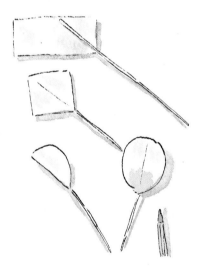

1 For each flower cut five 4 x 2in (10 x 5cm) rectangles from white crêpe paper to make petals. Spread glue across one half of a rectangle and place half a white stem wire diagonally across glued area. Crease paper over and press flat. Fold shape in half as shown and, using template as a guide, cut out petal shape.

2 Stretch petal between thumbs to cup base of petal and curve edges. Lightly colour-in lower half of each petal with pale green crayon.

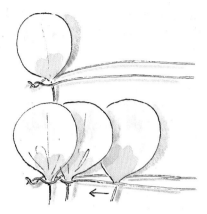

3 To join petals, take two pieces of binding wire and twist ends together as shown. Insert a petal and gather up base slightly. Hold firmly and twist wire to secure. Add more petals, overlapping them and making sure bases are level.

4 For flower centre, wrap and glue small scrap of cotton wool to end of a white wire flower stem. Cover with square of yellow tissue and secure with binding wire. Make four equally sized bunches of stamens. Arrange the stamens evenly around the yellow centre. Bind them tightly with wire.

5 Place the flower centre in the middle of the petals, wrapping petals around it. Use petal wires to secure parts together. Bind white flower tape over the petal bases and the stems.

Finishing the rose wreath

Attach the flower stems to the wreath by pushing stems in as far as possible. Twist wires to secure. Rearrange petals to shape.

Add holly leaves in same way, placing two at top of wreath and one to one side of base centre. Pull tendrils into shape, curving and opening them out.

Paper holly wreath

Copy this idea to make a quick and effective holly wreath, as shown on the right. Cut a circle from card, or use a flower-arranging foam ring as a base.

Crease leaf-size rectangles of green crêpe paper in half lengthways and cut out into spiky holly shapes.

For cardboard wreaths, attach each leaf base with sticky foam pads: for foam wreaths, use florists' pins or craft glue. Make berries from glued-on spots of shiny red foil and add at random. Complete the wreath with a few small red ribbons dotted amongst the holly and a large bow made from red crêpe paper.

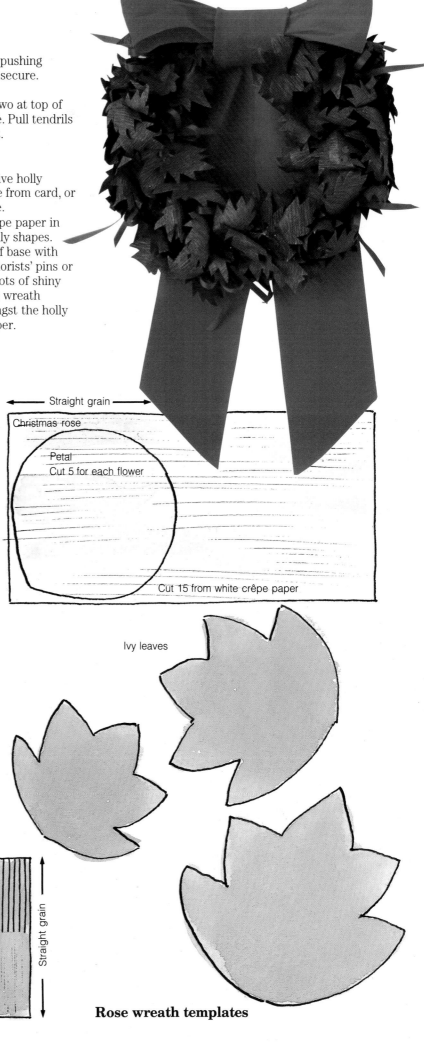

Straight grain

Christmas rose

Petal
Cut 5 for each flower

Cut 15 from white crêpe paper

Holly leaf
Cut 12 from green paper

Ivy leaves

Nuts   Cut 8 from green crêpe paper

Cut fringe

Straight grain

Rose wreath templates

Christmas crackers

*Handmade Christmas crackers add a
thoughtful touch to festive tree decorations and party table
settings. Surprisingly easy to make, crackers
can be designed to suit the occasion with tailor-made trims and
specially chosen gifts.*

One of the main advantages of making your own crackers is that you decide on the contents, so your friends and family will not be disappointed!

Besides adding a lavish finishing touch to your own decorations, a collection of beautifully boxed crackers would make a lovely family gift.

Materials and equipment

Papers Crêpe papers are most suitable for crackers, and they are available in many colours. The supporting linings are made from greaseproof paper (wax paper). The decorations can be made from paper-backed foil giftwrap, foil cake decorating bands, doilies, tissue paper, artist's cover papers, and giftwrap papers.

Thin card (card stock) is used to make cracker formers. These are card tubes which support the cracker as it is shaped. Thin, shiny or coloured card can also be used to make decorative trims.

Cracker contents such as snaps, jokes and mottos and printed paper scraps can be bought by mail order from specialist suppliers.

Party hats are also available, although it is easy to make your own from tissue paper.

Adhesive, like non-trailing stick adhesive, is ideal for sticking the papers together. Clear craft glue is used to stick the card formers.

Other materials Polypropylene parcel twine, scissors and pinking shears, pencil, rubber, small rubber bands. Optional materials include: gold spray, pearl beads and gold bead trimming, double sided sticky tape, plastic holly berries and other seasonal trims as desired.

Making a cracker

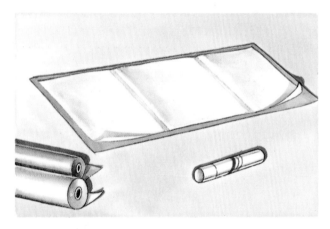

1 Cut a 6¼in (16cm) by 13¾in (35cm) rectangle of crêpe paper; cut with the grain running parallel to the longest sides. From greaseproof paper, cut a rectangle 6in (15cm) by 13½in (34cm). Using stick adhesive, draw a vertical line 4in (10cm) in from each end of the greaseproof paper. Stick it on the crêpe paper, leaving a ¼in (6mm) border all round.

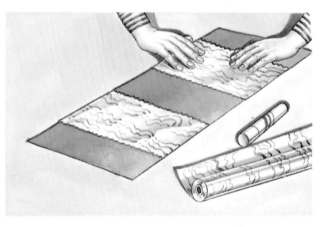

2 From foil giftwrap, cut two strips, each measuring 4in (10cm) by 6¼in (16cm). Trim along the longer sides with pinking shears. Use stick adhesive to attach the foil pieces, 2in (5cm) in from each end.

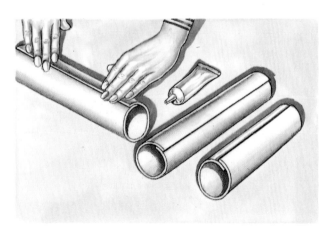

3 Make two cracker formers from two rectangles of thin card, each measuring 6in (15cm) by 8¼in (21cm). These will be the materials used to shape each cracker you make. Roll them into tubes, overlapping each edge by ½in (1.2cm). Use craft glue to hold. Cut another rectangle from card, measuring 4¾in (12cm) by 6in (15cm) and roll and glue into a tube shape as before.

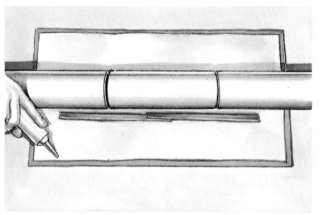

4 With wrong side of cracker facing, place the short card tube in the centre, and lay a cracker snap alongside, centres level. Place a former tube at each end, edges touching as shown. Run a thin line of craft glue along one long edge of crêpe paper, and roll up the cracker, rolling towards the glued overlap. Join, and leave until glue is dry.

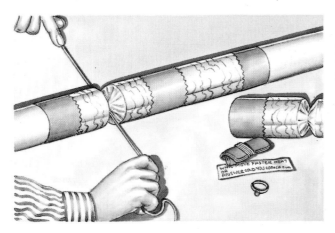

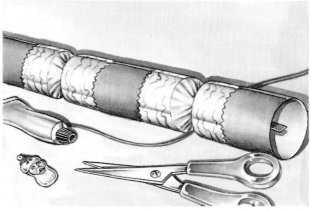

5 Pull out one former by 2in (5cm). Wrap a length of twine round the centre of the foil section, and pull the ends tightly to crimp the foil. When pulling the twine, keep it at right angles to the cracker to ensure a crisp, straight line. Remove the former and untie the twine.

6 Drop the gift, motto and hat (see instructions for making party hats) through the remaining former into the cracker. Pull out the former slightly, and crimp with twine as before. Remove former and twine. Now trim the cracker with a paper decoration.

Cracker decorations

As our opening picture shows, crackers can be given a variety of decorative seasonal treatments using papers, ribbons and beads. Trace the designs from the diagram and make paper templates so you can draw round the outlines directly on to the paper or card; or use well-worn carbon paper (so outline is soft) to transfer the designs from the tracing. Use clear craft glue to stick the decorations on to the crackers.

Holly decoration
Place leaf pattern on folded foil or green leatherette paper and cut out as many as required. Curl edges of leaves by gently stretching them over a scissor blade. Use clear adhesive to stick them to cracker, and to add a bunch of artificial berries to the centre of the leaves.

Mistletoe decoration
Cut leaf and stalk pattern from folded green cover paper. Fold base of leaves in line with stalk and curl over scissor blade as for holly. Glue three pearl beads to cracker, then glue ends of two mistletoe stalks between each bead.

Christmas rose
Cut rose pattern from thin white card and curl petals over a scissor blade. Stick a piece of double sided sticky tape to a scrap of card. Working in a spiral, press a length of gold bead trimming into the tape to make a ⅝in (1.5cm) circle. Cut round the outline and glue the card to the centre of the rose. Cut leaves from folded dark green cover paper. Glue roses and leaves to cracker.

Doily decorations
Lengths of foil cake banding, or borders cut from square doilies can be used to trim the edges of the crackers. Simply glue them across the short sides of the crêpe paper strip before the cracker is rolled.
To make a fan, cut a doily from edge to centre, and fold into accordian pleats. Taper folds slightly at the centre, and glue between pleats. To make a circular fan, glue the ends of two fans together.

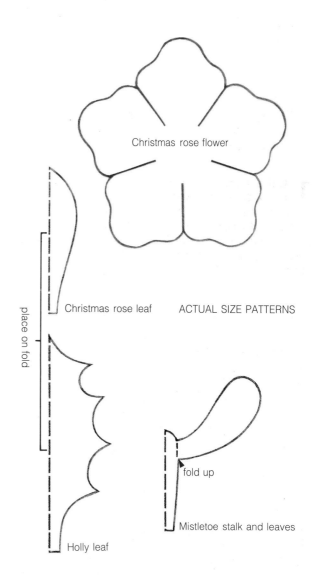

Christmas rose flower

place on fold

Christmas rose leaf   ACTUAL SIZE PATTERNS

fold up

Holly leaf

Mistletoe stalk and leaves

Making a paper hat

These can be made very quickly, and can be left plain or embellished with paper scraps, or beads and feathers. As the hat has to be rolled to fit into the cracker, choose trims that will roll without distorting or breaking.

You will need
◇ Tissue paper
◇ Stick adhesive
◇ Scissors
◇ Coloured papers
◇ Foil stickers
◇ Small rubber bands.

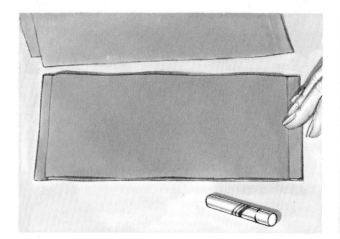

1 Cut two 4¾in (12cm) by 12½in (32cm) rectangles from tissue paper and use stick adhesive to join both short sides.

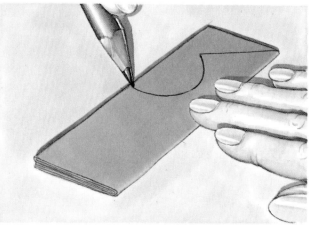

2 Fold hat in half, then half again, and then again to make eight equal sections. Draw a simple design at one end, and cut out through all layers.

3 Open out the hat and decorate with stickers, stars or other motifs. The designs can be added to the centre point, or applied all round the edge as desired.

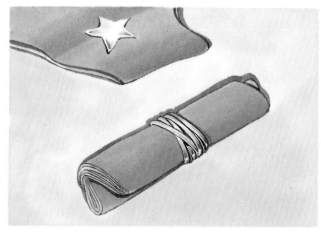

4 Re-fold the hat, then roll into a small parcel, taking care not to damage applied motifs. Secure with a rubber band, ready to insert into cracker.

ACTUAL SIZE PATTERN

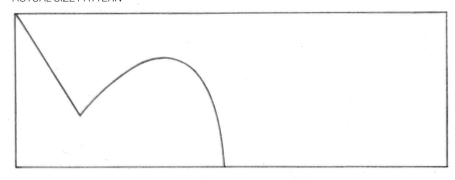

◁ *Fold the tissue paper into eight sections and draw a shaped design at one end, like the one shown here. Cut along the marked line and unfold, revealing the paper crown.*

Origami decorations

*Origami can be used to make beautiful seasonal
decorations. From one simple-to-fold base shape it is possible
to make designs that appear quite different.
Make them in one colour, or fold two contrasting shiny papers
together for a clever effect.*

The decorations pictured below are worked from a traditional origami windmill base. You can work the design to the windmill stage, and make a collection of windmills in bright colours to mount on sticks or hang as mobiles. Alternatively work the design a stage further for impressive pomander decorations.

As with most origami designs, these decorations are worked from a square of paper. This can vary in size as desired, but should measure at least 8¼in (21cm) square for easy handling.

Try out the designs using single sheets of paper, taking care to make each fold crisply and accurately. When you are more practised, work the decorations using two contrasting sheets of paper folded together wrong sides facing, for interesting two-tone effects.

You will need
◇ Squares of paper-backed foil papers, or other crisp-folding decorative paper
◇ Quick drying, non-trailing multi-purpose craft glue, or a stick adhesive
◇ Scissors
◇ Sticks and pins for making working windmills (optional)

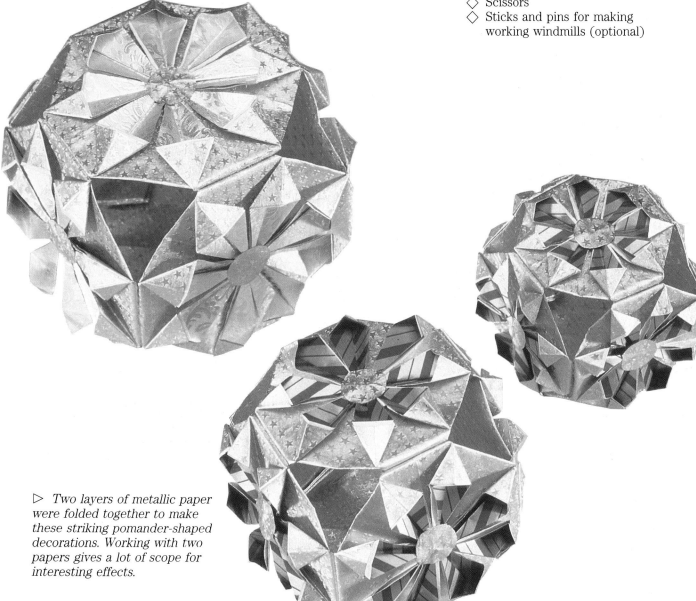

▷ *Two layers of metallic paper
were folded together to make
these striking pomander-shaped
decorations. Working with two
papers gives a lot of scope for
interesting effects.*

Making the basic shape

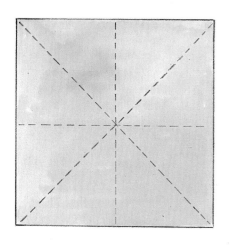

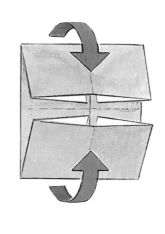

1 Fold and open out

2 Fold into centre

3 Fold to centre and unfold

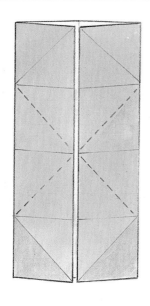

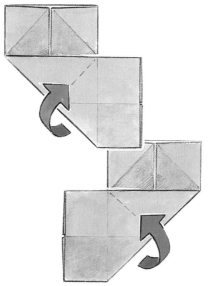

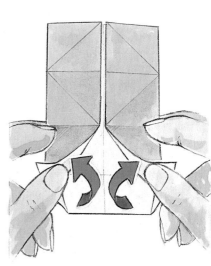

4 Crease as shown, step 5

5 Make creases

6 Lift corners up and out

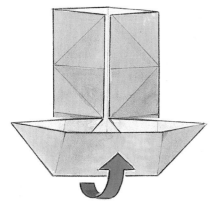

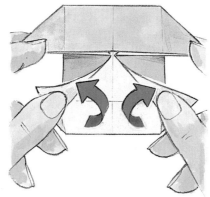

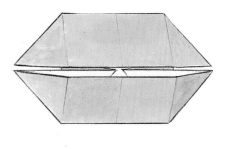

7 Fold up to centre

8 Turn upside down, repeat 6 and 7

9 This is the basic shape

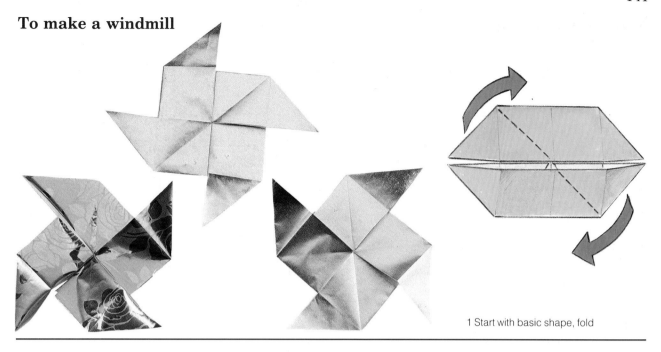

To make a windmill

1 Start with basic shape, fold

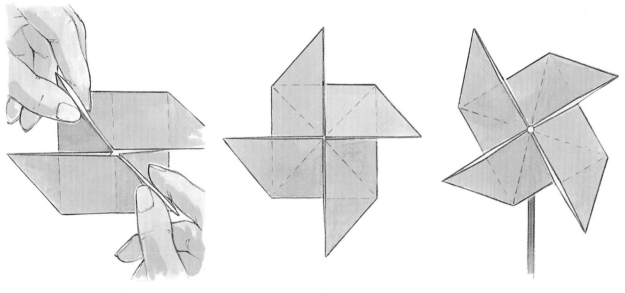

2 Fold up, fold down

3 The finished windmill

4 Fix centre to stick with pin or small nail. Blow to spin

To make a pomander

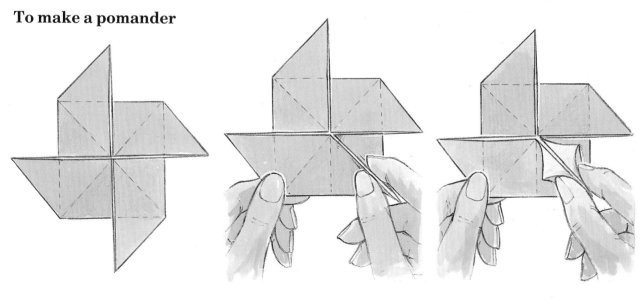

Start with windmill

2 Lift up

3 Push open

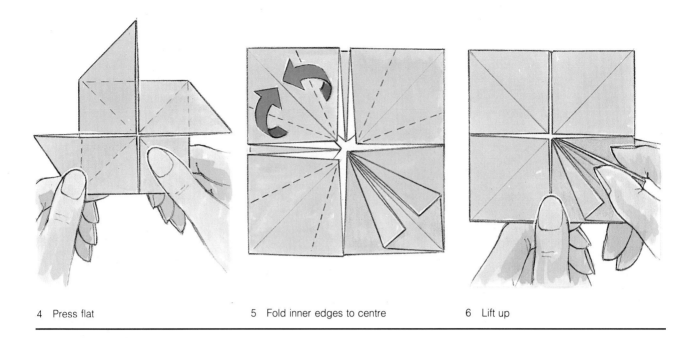

4 Press flat

5 Fold inner edges to centre

6 Lift up

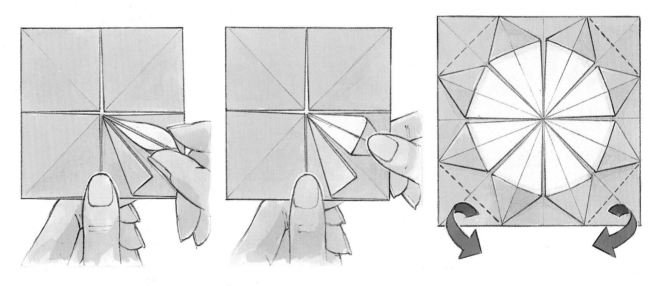

7 Open out

8 Press flat

9 Fold corners back

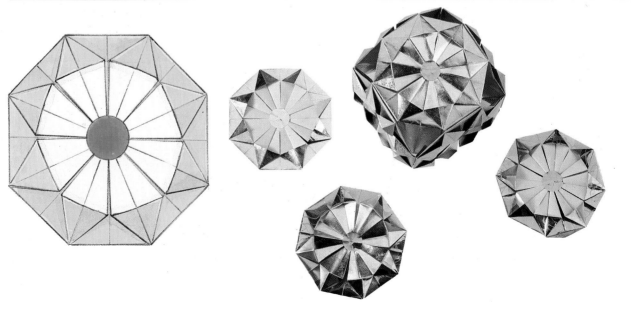

10 Stick paper circle to centre

11 Make six shapes and stick each together at corners to form the pomander

INDEX